NAPOLEON HILL
MY MENTOR

NAPOLEON HILL
MY MENTOR

Timeless Principles to Take Your Success to the Next Level

DON GREEN

CEO of the Napoleon Hill Foundation

MEDIA

Published 2021 by Gildan Media LLC
aka G&D Media
www.GandDmedia.com

Copyright © 2021 by The Napoleon Hill Foundation

Excerpts from *Napoleon Hill's Greatest Speeches* (The End of the Rainbow: 1922 Commencement Address at Salem College; and The Five Essentials of Success: 1957 Baccalaureate Sermon at Salem College), reprinted here courtesy of Sound Wisdom.

First Edition: 2021

Front cover design by David Rheinhardt of Pyrographx

Interior design by Meghan Day Healey of Story Horse, LLC.

Library of Congress Cataloging-in-Publication Data is available upon request

ISBN: 978-1-7225-0317-8

10 9 8 7 6 5 4 3 2 1

Contents

DON GREEN AT THE NAPOLEON HILL HISTORICAL MARKER

Foreword

by Dan Strutzel

This book will introduce to two unique individuals. The first is Oliver Napoleon Hill, whom most people know simply as Napoleon Hill. He was born on October 26, 1883, in the Appalachian town of Pound, Virginia, and died November 8, 1970. In those eighty-seven years, his accomplishments were legendary. He is probably best known for his world-renowned best seller, *Think and Grow Rich*, which is among the ten top selling self-help books of all time. The book contains many of the success secrets he learned as a result of a commission he received from steel magnate Andrew Carnegie to write the world's first philosophy of success. Hill quickly became a publishing powerhouse,

publishing more than ten best-selling books, numerous magazine articles, and courses.

The second individual, Don Green, was also born in an
Appalachian town—Stratton, Virginia—the son of a coal miner.
From a young age, Don had an entrepreneurial streak. His first
youthful business venture, at age fifteen, was charging admis-
sion to see his pet bear—yes, the living kind. After a series of
early business successes, he went on to become a CEO of a
savings and loan at the young age of forty-one. At that point it
was on the verge of being closed by federal banking authorities,
having lost capital of $1.5 million in the previous three years.

For the next eighteen years, while Don was the CEO, the
savings and loan, converted to a savings bank, was profitable
every single year. After the bank was sold and Don approached
the age of sixty, he was asked by the trustees of the Napoleon
Hill Foundation to become executive director and manage the
foundation's affairs on a daily basis.

Since Don's background was in banking, he had little knowledge of book publishing. Nevertheless, he had many years of
experience as a banker and as owner of several businesses in
various fields, from real estate development to dry cleaning.
This, along with his love for books and learning, particularly the
works of Napoleon Hill, led him to take the foundation's work to
a new level of success.

You might say that Don Green, CEO of the Napoleon Hill
Foundation to this day, succeeded by applying the principles
that his mentor Napoleon Hill discussed in his many publica-

tions. In this book, you'll develop a deeper understanding of both of these outstanding individuals.

I have had the privilege of knowing both of these great men—one indirectly, through his many great written works and powerful speeches, and the other directly, though a long-standing working relationship that spans over fifteen years. As the former VP of Nightingale-Conant Corporation, many years ago I had the honor of helping to produce and publish some of Napoleon Hill's classic audio titles. It was then that I began to work with Don Green, in negotiating business deals to expand the reach of the Napoleon Hill content around the world. I have continued and deepened that work with Don, since forming Inspire Productions in 2014, so together we could continue to build upon the Napoleon Hill publishing legacy. And I can say, first hand, that Don Green is the very definition of every quality of personality that Napoleon Hill discussed—a man of the utmost integrity, professionalism, candor and wisdom.

Not only will Don discuss the principles of success that made Napoleon Hill famous, but he'll also share some of his personal knowledge of Hill, including stories and insights about him that haven't been publicly mentioned before.

Best of all, Don Green will convince you that the principles behind Napoleon Hill's classics like *Think and Grow Rich*, written more than eighty years ago, are more vital and relevant than ever. He'll teach you the principles by outlining those that have been most important to him and will give you practical ways to put the power of Napoleon Hill to work for you.

You'll learn the tools needed to uncover the secrets of growth, creativity, power, and achievement inside all of us. These are essential for any business professional seeking the knowledge and inspiration necessary to discard fear and obtain personal and professional triumph. If you're ready to apply Hill's time-tested tools for success and make your dreams a reality, then keep reading. You're about to hear about how these two individuals, both born in rural Appalachian towns and who started out with few financial resources, went on to live the American dream.

If they can do it, you certainly can go on to live your dreams as well.

Dan Strutzel is the President of Inspire Productions, and the former Executive VP of Publishing at Nightingale-Conant Corporation. He has published some of the most successful audio programs in history. Dan is a twenty-eight-year veteran of the personal development industry, and has worked "up close and personal" with several hundred authors and speakers—including Tony Robbins, Brian Tracy, Jim Rohn, Denis Waitley, Marianne Williamson, Harvey Mackay, Deepak Chopra, Robert Kiyosaki, Wayne Dyer and Zig Ziglar. Dan is the author of *30 Days to a More Powerful Vocabulary, 30 Days to a More Powerful Business Vocabulary*, and *The Top 1%*, published by G&D Media. Dan is a graduate of The University of Notre Dame.

ONE

Coal Miner's Son

I have a passion for what I do and for the results that I've obtained through the lives of others. I originated a course I called "Keys to Success." I did not want to use *Think and Grow Rich*; I let people think the course was just about money. There were seventeen principles that people could use and apply in daily life.

My first class was a night class. I had a lady in there who was a CPA, but she wanted to be an attorney, doing legal work for corporations because she already knew the tax structures. I saw her recently, and she said, "Don, I've been wanting to run into you. The other day I was looking at my paper from when I was in your class. I said my goal was to become a corporate attorney. You wrote at the bottom, 'Don't tell me. Go out and do it.'"

I love stories from young people in my classes. They went out in the world and became CPAs or business owners. Once they get that inspiration, almost nothing can hold them back. I've had young people in my classes, but I've also had older people, including farmers as well as medical doctors.

In the end, it comes down to how badly you really want to succeed. These students wanted it bad. Many have started with no opportunities in life. It's no reflection on their parents. Most of our parents did the best they could with what they had. For these students to have opportunity and to make the most of it is very rewarding, because I realize that some of them are the first generation of their families to go to college. When I went to college and graduated, I knew that when my daughter came along, she would be going to college. When a grandson was born, the first thing I did was to buy him a four-year college education. It becomes an assumption: we assume that our descendants are going to follow in our path. I think that's how we cure poverty.

Many people born in poverty just accept it. For instance, one day I was talking to a man whose son was going to school with my daughter. I said, "Of course, your son is going to college." He used some choice words and then said, "He's not going nowhere. It's too expensive." I came back at him and said, "It's not nearly as expensive as ignorance."

Many times kids just need a little encouragement. They may have grown up in homes in which people told them over and over again that they're not prepared for life, so they don't realize their potential.

Two Ways of Learning

We learn two ways: from associating with people and from books. If we don't listen to someone else, we don't stand a very good chance of getting ahead in life. We accept certain things as fate, even though we can change them. But reading and association with other people rub off on you.

I read many books. Sometimes you only pick up one idea, something that you want to jot down, or you read a book and it refers to another book. You make a note to order that book to see what the author of the first one learned from it. Education is a lifelong process. I've told the students a thousand times, "Just think of an education as a bridge. It's a bridge to take you from where you are to where you want to go." It's just that simple, but you have to have some means to get there. If you accept what you were dealt with, that you were born in poverty, your parents are in poverty, and all they ever knew was poverty, you will just accept your fate.

Somewhere along the line I noticed that most people start making excuses: "My parents didn't send me to the right school; my taxes are too high; there are no opportunities." I published a little book called *Your Greatest Power: The Choice Is Yours* by J. Martin Kohe, a psychologist that our founding chairman, Mr. W. Clement Stone, worked with. It's sold more than a million copies. It's only ninety-six pages, but it explains the power we have to choose. This is the greatest power that we all have.

The concept of "two envelopes" illustrates the principle of choice. Napoleon Hill spoke about this in a 1955 radio program. He said that at the time of our birth, each of us brings with him the equivalent of two sealed envelopes. One contains a list of riches that we may enjoy by taking possession of our minds and using them to attain what we desire in life. The other envelope contains a list of penalties that nature will exact from us if we neglect to recognize and use our mind power.

You got up this morning and decided to read this book. You could have gone out hunting or done drugs or stayed home and watched soap operas. We have that ability to make that choice. The choices we make become habits. Habits in turn define who we are, good or bad. Our minds will accept positive information; they'll also accept negative information. The thought we dwell on the most is the one we're most likely to become.

Early Years

I was born in 1941, a son of a coal miner who was born in 1917. He married my mom, who was then two months short of fourteen years old (often young girls got married early looking for a better life). Mom was from a family of sixteen children, all of whom lived to reach maturity, with several of them, including my mom, living into their nineties. Both of my parents had seventh-grade educations. My mother said that even the teacher had only a seventh-grade education. My oldest brother was born when mom was sixteen, and before she was twenty-two, she had given birth to four sons. A daughter was born to her at the age of twenty-seven.

My parents lived through the Great Depression, but my dad was never unemployed or sought federal assistance, even during one period for months after a life-threatening accident that occurred when he was working as an underground miner. His back was broken in a rock fall, and he could not walk without crutches. Underground miners made about $6 a day. Workman's comp was $15 a week. Instead of drawing compensation, Dad took a job driving a coal truck at $5 per day until his wounds healed to the point where the company doctor released him to work in the mine.

I recall as a youngster seeing Mom following Dad to the truck, with him on crutches, then seeing him climb up into the truck. Mom would hand up the crutches and the lunch that she'd packed for him. (It never occurred to me to ask how he went to the bathroom during the day.) He took a lot of pride in being self-reliant and providing for a wife and five children.

My parents taught me about work. My mom said a thousand times, "Hard work never killed nobody." She was full of sayings like, "You can't spend money you don't got," "Don't let a little money burn a hole in your pocket," "It takes money to ride a train," and plenty of other sayings to try to keep us on track. She said, "You cannot waste your money. Your daddy crawls around in that old hole, and you never know when he might get hurt or even get killed." I recall hearing things like, "If you tell people what you're going to do, just be sure you do as you told them." If you got a whipping in school, you got another when you get home, because your parents knew the teacher was right.

I loved to read books, especially biographies. When I got to the eighth grade, we had a librarian by the name of Miss Barr, who seemed to protect the books with her own life. She would not let you check out more than one at a time. One book might have been enough, except during weekends or school closings because of weather, but I solved this problem. I can remember it just like yesterday, even though it was about sixty-five years ago. There were twins that worked in the library at different times of the day. They were older than me. I could not tell them apart, but they were both beautiful. I was in love with them, but I'm afraid it was one-sided. Anyway, I would get one book. I'd put it in my locker, go back later in the day between classes, and check out another book when the other twin was working. It was a beautiful deal.

I can still recall my mom saying, "I swear you're going to go blind from reading so much." I would put down the book for maybe a minute or two, and I'd pick it back up again. I just couldn't stay away from books. It's not hard to understand why I support reading and have given away thousands of books, and I still do today. One day, while I was visiting my mom, who was then in her eighties or early nineties, she said, "Don, someone is always telling me about the books you gave to the kids. Do you guess they read them?" I said, "Mom, I hope so, because this kid read them, and it's made a world of difference in my life."

Yes, if one reads them and is inspired, it was worthwhile.

Work in Finance

When I was about twenty-one, I took a job with a consumer finance agency at the minimum wage of $1.15 per hour, and I was one happy young lad. I had my own business card that read "assistant manager," but in reality I was outside collecting on a daily basis. I went into the office and was handed a route that contained twenty or more cards showing people's names, addresses, places of employment, payment schedules, collateral (if any), the amounts due, and the names of the signers of the loan.

I was already into books and tapes, which were audiocassettes at the time. Except for the many stops, I was sitting in my old car all day long. I would read from the self-help leaders— Napoleon Hill, Zig Ziglar, Denis Waitley, Ed Foreman, and others. Although I was making $1.15 an hour, with less than 60 cents for overtime. I never complained. I was still happy because I was furnishing myself with educational material, which I knew was going to take me places.

For the use of the car, I was paid $.075 per mile. Phyl, my wife, packed sandwiches, usually peanut butter and jelly or bologna. It was a treat for me to be able to stop and get a Pepsi or something to drink. I invested in other cassettes and books, and I quickly learned Napoleon Hill was born in Wise County, which was our home. He was a favorite because it seemed all of the others had learned from him.

Not only did I read Hill's books and listen to his voice, but I tried to read the books he read, especially by the authors he quoted from, like Orison Swett Marden, Samuel Smiles, Elbert Hubbard, John Dewey, Ella Wheeler Wilcox, William James, James Allen, and Ralph Waldo Emerson. (Hill used Emerson's essay "Compensation" as material.) I still have a copy of Dewey's *How We Think*, which was published in 1910.

Like Hill, Marden had read Samuel Smiles. Marden had two degrees, one in medicine and one in law, from Harvard. He wrote such books as *An Iron Will*, *Every Man a King*, and *Pushing to the Front*. He was also the founder of *Success* magazine in 1897.

Samuel Smiles had written a book called *Self-Help* in 1859. I believe that was the first self-help book. He wrote about people who practiced persistence, such as James Watt, who perfected the steam engine. He also wrote about Josiah Wedgwood, who spent years and years to perfect the famous Wedgwood china.

Like Hill, Smiles wrote about people overcoming adversity, but whereas Smiles simply got stories from newspapers or other sources and put them in his own words, Hill went out and actually interviewed them on a one-on-one basis. Hill saw over five hundred people, and I think it made a lot of difference. In any event, my interest in Napoleon Hill and success followed me through my whole career.

In the consumer finance business, I think I got the best training in the world, because I learned what *not* to do. People said, "We'll use the money for food, clothing, and shelter to live the good life." It's not that they didn't make money, it's just that they never learned to take care of it. Most of them didn't plan on failing; they just failed to plan.

My dad never had a debt problem. He built a nice brick house and paid for it with $4,000, the most money he ever borrowed in his life. He did not believe in going out and buying things on credit. He took care of our money. Yet at the same time, we supported the church and other things. I learned a lot from him.

My career started out with the desire to make money, because my father worked in underground coal mines, which is a very dangerous profession. Apart from roof collapses and heavy machinery, miners often developed a disease called black lung, which came from breathing the coal dust. Back then, the life expectancy of a miner was about twenty years less than in other professions.

My parents provided food, clothing, and shelter, but they were thrifty by necessity. Often when as a child I'd ask for money, I was told, "Honey, we cannot waste our money. Your poor dad crawls around in the mines." Often I was told, "Nothing can replace the thrill of knowing you earned your own money." This made it easy to practice thrift and do some soul-searching before spending money that you earned. Teaching youngsters how to save money is a valuable lesson, even if they do not need the money. Teaching them to appreciate money is a lesson that will markedly last a lifetime and pay bountiful rewards.

The Snake Pit

At one point I operated a snake pit. I knew there were places where they displayed snakes and sold them in Silver Springs, Florida. Once on a vacation, Dad had a friend who was mostly Indian, by the name of Bates. He caught snakes, and he took my dad; I even went with them.

Then we learned to catch them ourselves. It's really not hard. They were rattlesnakes and copperheads, and we put them in a duffel bag. There was a little building by the road that was used to sell apples for a family orchard. We made a pit eight or ten feet deep, with a concrete bottom. We turned the snakes loose in it. We made little signs up: "25 cents to see the reptiles; 10 cents for children under 10."

I had an older friend who drove a Royal Crown Cola truck. He had big signs that said "Royal Crown Cola," but at the bottom, they had a white strip where you could put your business's name. We painted "Indian Mountain Reptile Garden ahead" on the strips and we put them on each side of the road. Back in those days, we got no permits; we just stuck the money in our pockets. Then Dad built a little building out of rough lumber of around 10 by 16 feet. We put a pop machine outside.

At first, we started selling snacks—potato chips and crackers. We added some more souvenirs. I went to a place about a two-hour drive down close to Cumberland Gap, where there was a place where you could buy souvenirs. We would buy ash trays for cigarettes. They were a quarter apiece, and they had comics on them. To make souvenirs out of them, all you had to do was to buy little stick-on signs that said "Indian Mountain Reptile Garden, U.S. 23" and put them on. You could sell them for a dollar. Lots of days when I sold souvenirs, I would make more than $100. If you're fifteen or sixteen years old, that's a lot of money. Of course, it was a very short season, starting when we got out of school, and it practically died around Labor Day, because people weren't traveling after that point.

With this business, I learned a lot more than I did in school. People would identify themselves by saying, "I work with your dad in the mines." In the summertime, they'd come and stop, and there would one or two cars following them with out-of-state tags. We lived in a rural area, where there's not a lot of entertainment. It always seemed that anytime they had relatives visiting, they would bring them to the snake pit. (Of course, I'd also added a bear, monkeys, skunks, bobcats, and exotic birds.) They would bring people, and they'd tell me, "I brought you my brother-in-law, who's coming here from Ohio on vacation."

I'd say, "Next time you bring somebody here, you could do me a favor and show them around. I won't charge you the quarter to get in." They were all coal miners, and they were in heaven to be able to get up on stage. Then they would say, "I've got to buy something to take back." It was nothing for them to spend $20, $30, $40, $50, or more on souvenirs. I think I learned how to treat people by saying, "Hey, do me a favor." They loved doing it. I gave up a quarter for them to show other people around. Nobody had to teach that to me. It just seemed to be a common thing to do, plus I enjoyed it, every minute of it. This was my first big entrepreneurial venture.

Business Enterprises

I also had my own real estate development company. Most of the wealth that made this country has been made in real estate. I learned to buy something and pay for it. I saw a lot of people make mistakes: they would buy a lot by borrowing the money. But if an investment doesn't return the income, it'll become an alligator. It'll eat you alive.

I also started a dry cleaning business. I had already started in banking, and I wore a suit every day. I was not pleased with the results I got from the cleaners. I spent $39.95 on a little kit I saw advertised in *Inc.* magazine, which showed how to operate a dry cleaners. I studied and studied it. I pitched the idea to a couple of friends. It's an easy business to run. I added one-day service and a drive-in so that you didn't have to get out of the car—things that people really wanted.

In the area, we had three old, outdated dry cleaners. They had stuff stacked all over the floor; it looked as if it had been there for years. So we operated in the modern way. We had tile on the floor and a nice granite counter. If you stopped in for your first time, I would give you a bag to put your clothes in, and the clerk would write on it, "Shirts folded for travel" or "light starch" or "no starch." The bag had the business's name—"The Cleaners"—on it. That was us. We never spent a nickel for advertising—no ads, no coupons.

We charged more than the other people did, but we gave one-day service. I talked to a lady who had worked years for another place; when I told her I was going to do one-day service, she said, "You can't do that."

"Let me ask you something," I said. "Say someone comes by here and drops off a couple of suits and four white shirts. You take them back, and you give them to the employees to start working on right now. How long does it take to do the shirts? I'm talking about washing them, starching them, ironing them, and putting them up."

"About three hours," she said

"How about the suits?"

"About the same."

"So," I said, "why don't we do them as quickly as we get them? I know what you've been used to, because I've been in the place where you worked. They throw the stuff on the floor for three or four days. Then somebody says, 'This has got to go out tomorrow,' and then they start working on it."

The woman never believed it would happen, but she agreed. I didn't know how to do anything at a cleaner, but I knew how to treat people.

I happened to be in there one Saturday when some young kids brought their band uniforms in. School was starting. I told the kids, "We're not going to charge you for doing your uniforms. You can tell the other kids we'll do the uniforms for free."

Once they left, the clerk said, "You'll go broke."

"Believe me," I said, "we've got money. We know what we're doing. You just do your job and learn from it, because here's what's going to happen. Not all of them will appreciate it, but many will tell their parents, 'Mom, you can't believe it. They didn't charge me for cleaning my uniform.' If they're not our customers already, chances are, they're going to be."

One day I went in and said, "When people come in who have had a death in the family, don't charge them anything."

Again she came back: "Are we trying to go broke?"

"No," I said, "we're not going to go broke. Did your paycheck ever bounce? We've got money, and we're making money. Many people will reward us; some of them won't, but that's their problem."

Some people just never learned that. I guess it's the way I was raised. It just seemed to be natural to do somebody a favor if it doesn't break you. I looked at it as an investment. That was a better form of advertising, because lawyers, for example, talk to one another. They'd tell each other they could drop their clothes off, go and spend a day in court, and come back and pick them up.

I can remember one in particular: I didn't see his name on my list of customers. One day I saw him and said, "Greg, I'm not seeing you using my cleaners."

"Well," he said, "my wife can't do my clothes, but I learned to do them when I was in the army."

"Greg," I said, "let me tell you something. You do some legal work for me." I believe he was charging $75 or $100 an hour. "Instead of doing your own clothes, you should be working where you make the most money."

"I got it." he said. He started using us and told everybody how much time he was saving by not having to do his clothes on the weekends.

Banking

As for my banking career, I worked for a company called Time Finance (later it was CIT) in the coal fields, and they had about a dozen offices in northern Appalachia, with one supervisor looking over all of them.

The guys who had been around a while called me "hotshot," because I had a lot of energy. I was twenty-one years old, and those guys had been managers for a long time. They probably weren't going anywhere. Our supervisor was telling me about an office opening up in Indianapolis. CIT had bought two or three little companies and put them together, so there would probably be some openings.

They offered me Plainfield, Indiana, which is outside of Indianapolis. It was a small office in a little shopping center. I only had one clerk working for me. She'd been there, and she knew the customers. I just did what I knew: seek a new customer by being friendly to people and making it easy for them to borrow money. In no time the office was in tremendous shape. In my early twenties, I was the youngest branch manager in CIT history.

Then there was an office in downtown Indianapolis. It's across from Eli Lilly, the drug manufacturer. The previous manager had died, so they offered me that office. It was in bad shape in regard to delinquencies and other matters. We had a meeting once a month with all the branch managers.

When I took this office, the guys were talking. They said, "Boy, whoever does Don's office out there in Plainfield is going to have it made. He had such a good office." Others said, "No, they will have it rough, because they're going to be judged by what he has done."

I took over this second office and did tremendously. When I started, they suggested that the manager should get 50 percent of the points for a new customer, for a former customer, for growth in loans outstanding. The other 50 percent would be divided up among other employees.

I held a staff meeting in which I said, "The first thing we're going to do is rewrite the rules. They didn't say we had to split the points this way. It was a suggestion. So we're going to split the points evenly."

I went to a managers' meeting in Louisville, Kentucky; there were maybe three or four hundred people, and I was sitting towards the back. The president said, "Would Don Green come forward?" They wanted to know how I did it. I said, "*I* didn't. *We* did it." It's something I learned a long time ago: I've never had anybody working for me. I have people working *with* me. It makes all the difference in the world.

I've seen guys sit down and do a budget and say, "This is what I'm going to do." But I ask the employees: "Dan, what do you think we could do this month? John, what do you think we can do here?" Normally they will set higher goals than I would set myself, but the important thing is, they're part of it; they've bought into it.

You don't get a whole lot by ordering people around. Instead you get them working with you and seeing that you're all going to win from it, not just one guy at the top. Sometimes people, especially when they are promoted early, think they have a lot of control, and they can act like dictators: "You do this, you do that." And the employees are thinking, "I will while you're watching me, but when you're not . . ."

Motivational speaker Zig Ziglar once told me that when he was in a factory, he asked one of the workers, "How long have you been working here?" The worker said, "Ever since they threatened to fire me." I think that's a big part of this attitude: "You get the big salary, so I'll do just enough to get by." But when employees buy into it, you've got a whole different organization.

At one point, I saw an ad seeking a consumer finance manager. I made contact with them and took a job in Kingsport, Tennessee. It was owned by a large consumer finance agency, which had lots of offices all over. They gave me a job, so I moved back from Indianapolis. Although I changed companies, I was never laid off in my entire life, and I was never without employment.

A new bank opened up in Wise County, Virginia, which is an hour or so away from where I was living. A man by the name of James A. Brown called me. He started a bank when he was twenty-nine. He's a mentor today. I spent six hours with him a couple weeks ago; I just love him. He has done so well; you can write stories and stories about him. Anyway, he said the bank was a year old. They had had some difficulties, and my name came up. He would like to interview me. He said, "Would you come over one day?"

"Well, Jim," I said, "the people I work for have been really good to me. I've got a four-year degree, and I'm getting ready to sign up to get a master's. I know I'm getting promoted. I'll end up being treasurer—a higher position. It has always been my dream to get into banking, but I can't come during the week."

"Why not?"

"Well, sir, these people are paying me. I'll come on a Saturday or Sunday if you want."

He said OK, so we set up a time when I went to his office. I remember him telling me, "You know, if you work a little harder, if you try a little more one day, probably nobody would notice it. If you do that for a week, still probably nobody would know it, but if you continue to do a little bit more than everybody around you, you're going to be a success that other people are only going to dream about." I still remember that. That was in 1975.

He gave me a job, and I was the second person in the bank. They had a data processing company in Knoxville, Tennessee, which issued their monthly reports. I was only there for a few days when I saw them emptying out some cards. I asked one of the clerks what those were.

She said, "Those are people that are delinquent."

"What do you all do with them?"

"We throw them away."

It took me a little while working until midnight to stay in there and get these cards lined up. I broke people down into who was six months past due and so on. I wrote a series of collection letters to send out to these people, each one getting a little bit firmer.

At the time I started, the bank was under cease and desist orders, which meant that they couldn't increase loans outstanding to people; they had severe restrictions on them.

The examiners came back about a year later, and they said it was hard to believe they were in the same bank. In fact Jim came to my office and asked me to come to the board meeting; he called me into the boardroom, although I was not a director.

Before I left, I got the best raise I ever got, because I was results-oriented. We sold out after I'd been in the bank for seven years, and today it's part of Bank of America. Jim protected me in the sellout.

Then I got a good position as a commercial loan officer. Quite a bit more money. I worked for them a year, and I really enjoyed it. When the little savings and loan was available, they had interviewed several people who turned them down, because they were closing S&Ls all over the place in the eighties.

I sat down with a pad and of course asked for a contract. I filled up a sheet of things I wanted and they all signed it, except for one trustee. Later the other trustees said that I was the best banker in the state of Virginia. We made $90,000 the first year, the second year around $300,000, and we got to where we were making $1 million a year.

I used the same principle. I had three people working for me. One day I had lunch with a trustee who was a major stockholder, and I said, "I would like to give all the employees a raise."

"We can't afford that now, Don."

I said, "I'm not talking about myself. They've been there three years without getting a raise, and we're going to make the money."

They did get the raise. I never asked for a raise. I knew what the other guys were making in town, because I had their houses financed. I knew what their salaries were. I was roughly making what the other three made.

I used the same ideas that I learned growing up: treat the employees well. I didn't have a turnover in personnel, because I treated them well, and I looked out for them. If you look out for the employees, they're going to look out for you. To me, these are just simple lessons. You can accomplish more by being good to people. They sense it if you're going to take care of them, because you always have.

The Book Business

When I started out with the Napoleon Hill Foundation, our chairman was Charlie Johnson, who passed away in 2019 at age eighty-five. He was Hill's nephew, and he referred to him as Uncle Nap. Hill had married his mother's sister. He said, "Don, I just didn't know if you knew anything about the book business."

"Charlie," I said, "it's all about people; books are what we work with. If we work with dry cleaning or loaning money or no matter what, I can do almost nothing, but I could find people that can do things for me, and they're glad to, because I'm going to treat them well, with respect, time off, with benefits or salary increases."

I learned a long time ago the best investments we ever make is what we invest in ourselves. The second best is our investments in our employees and our family. It's just that plain and simple: treating people well, in working together, and not having somebody working for you but working with you. It doesn't sound like a big deal, but it is to the person who's in that position.

How did I get to be involved with the Napoleon Hill Foundation? Of course I was reading his works, because I knew he was from the area. I used his statement that sometimes our ship *doesn't* come in; in a word, if there's not an opportunity, you create an opportunity.

I was invited to come and have lunch with W. Clement Stone. He was the head of a huge insurance company, which today is called Aon. He lived to be a hundred. Back then, he was responsible for the foundation. He lent it $500,000 to get it going and to publish books. He charged them no interest, and when they started publishing the books, they paid him back. He was our chairman until he died.

He invited me to come up to Chicago. He had some friends in the airline industry who had a boardroom at O'Hare airport, so we met there. I got there early. I saw him walking down, and he had two people with him; I think one was a nurse. He was probably around eighty, and he had a little mustache and wore gold cufflinks.

We talked and talked, and he said, "Boy, you know more about these books than I do. You ought to be a board member."

"What do I need to do, Mr. Stone?"

"Just tell us yes, and we'll give you the reports and keep you up with what's going on." That's how it came about. We create our own opportunities.

I sat on the board for numerous years before the foundation started looking for a new CEO to replace the previous one, who couldn't travel. They told me, "Don, you know more about the foundation than anybody."

"Yes," I said, "but I don't want to live in Chicago."

They said, "You can move it down to where you're living."

"I can do that?"

"All we need to do is transfer the accounts."

I bought a phone and a fax machine, and I was in business. At that point, they weren't doing any foreign business except with Japan. There was no Internet. I got a book that contained a list of international publishers. It listed their names, their addresses and their fax and phone numbers (they had no email in those days) as well as how many books they had published the previous year. It also listed the genres they published in, such as self-help, medical, or education. I picked out ones that seemed to be publishing the type of books we do. Then I wrote to them, describing our books to see if they were interested. I started getting replies, sometimes by mail and sometimes by fax.

At this point, I don't even know how many publishers we're connected with; I just know it's more than five hundred. We have twenty-five different Russian publishers, somewhere in the thirties in China, somewhere in the forties in Spanish. We've also done books in Macedonia, Iran, Afghanistan, Cyprus, Greece, Turkey, Slovenia, Slovakia, and Poland among many others.

One day—it was a Friday—my assistant, Zane, came back and said to me, "Don, this man on the phone wants to talk to you; he says he's in Iran." The man was from Iran but had worked and lived in the United States. He said, "I would like to publish a book by Napoleon Hill." At that time a few years back, we didn't have publications in Iran.

"I'll tell you what," I said. "I'll give you rights to the book for five years for a $2,000 advance." I probably could have gotten a lot more money, but I couldn't be sure that he would have gone for it. He gave me his name and address. Zane sent it on to Bob, our attorney.

Bob prepared the contract on the same day, and I signed it. Zane scanned it and emailed it to that guy in Iran with banking and wire transfer and instructions. We got the $2,000 on Monday.

It's hard to explain what a good feeling that is. I feel the same way about Saudi Arabia. We have published at least twenty-five different books in Saudi Arabia. I did a book with Sharon Lechter called *Think and Grow Rich for Women*, and the first foreign country that bought rights was Saudi Arabia.

It thrilled Sharon. I'm not saying we take credit for it, but since we've been doing business over there, women can attend sporting events and drive automobiles. That may not be a big deal to people living in the United States, but, believe me, to those ladies in Saudi Arabia, I would say that it is a big deal. We don't teach our course in Saudi Arabia, but we have taught it in Dubai and Egypt and some of the other neighboring countries.

I would like to have our course taught in Iran. It would be great if they could use Napoleon Hill's ideas to work things out together, because as a whole, we human beings all have the same desires. We want our children to be better off than we are. We want security and protection. We may be of different religions, we may be of different skin colors, but we're all humans, and we're all really brothers and sisters.

One of the best pieces Hill wrote many years ago was entitled "Intolerance." He wanted an end to intolerance. He said he looked forward to the day when we would know one another as brothers and sisters, not as Jews or Gentiles or as other such categories.

The Philosophy of Success

As the CEO of Napoleon Hill Foundation, I'm often asked what I think makes Hill's philosophy so unique. Why does it resonate with people around the globe?

Hill was bothered by one simple thing: why are some people successful and others not? He wanted to work with someone from whom he thought he could learn the most, so he took a job as a secretary for the noted Virginia attorney Rufus Ayers for $50 a month.

Ayers was called General Rufus Ayers, although he was not a general in the Confederate Army; he had joined when he was just fourteen. He came out and read a lot and truly was a success story. He was in both the coal and the lumber businesses, and he ended up as attorney general for the State of Virginia.

Napoleon saw how successful Ayers was, so he decided he would become a lawyer. He talked to his brother Vivian, and they applied to law school at Georgetown University. They were admitted, although Napoleon never finished.

Napoleon then worked writing newspaper articles. As a cub reporter, he covered Wright Brothers flights. He also worked for Bob Taylor, who was a governor of Tennessee and also a U.S. senator. People say he was one of the best speakers in the Senate.

In 1908, Hill was assigned to interview Andrew Carnegie. Carnegie challenged him to develop a philosophy of success, and he accepted. Napoleon said he had to go to the library, because he didn't know what the word *philosophy* meant.

From his childhood, Hill had always been a dreamer. His mother died when he was only eight, but his father remarried. Napoleon's stepmother's previous husband been a high-school principal, and her father was a doctor, so naturally she stressed education. She took a liking to the young Napoleon, even though he was somewhat mischievous. Later he said about her—much as Lincoln said about his stepmother—"Anything I ever am or aspire to be I owe to that dear woman." He said that oftentimes she was the only one on his side, the only one who was encouraging him.

Hill had persistence. He followed the principle that "it's not how many times you get knocked down. It's how many times you get back up."

You could say that Hill made mistakes, but when things go wrong, you can look at them either as failures or as learning lessons, as stumbling blocks or as stepping-stones.

It all starts with a burning desire or personal goal. Hill talked about how we develop faith. It starts with a burning desire and a goal that we want with a passion, followed by plans and then action. Action is faith that you start with and stick with. It's applied faith. It's not only believing you can achieve a goal but doing something about it.

Andrew Carnegie only had a few years of formal education. He worked as a bobbin boy in a textile mill, but there was a colonel who furnished books for the boys. They could go by on Saturdays and get books to read, and Carnegie read about Western civilization. By age thirty, he had become a millionaire by investing some earnings into sleeping cars.

If you read the stories of Carnegie or Napoleon Hill, you think, "If they did it, maybe I can do it too." I think that's why we read these stories—to get inspired.

It relates to the Roger Bannister story. Before 1954, practically everyone said it was impossible to run a mile in under four minutes. Then a British medical student named Roger Bannister did it. Now even high school boys run the mile in less than four minutes.

I think this proves that something is impossible only until somebody does it; then people accept it. The only limitations we have are those we set up ourselves. I think it's still true today. There are many stories of people who have accomplished a goal simply because they had a belief system saying they could succeed at it.

Andrew Carnegie selected Napoleon Hill to study and write about successful individuals, but he'd offered the same idea to lots of other people. The story was that when he asked Hill whether he would he take on the project, Carnegie was holding a stopwatch under his desk and gave him sixty seconds. About half of that time had gone by when Napoleon said he would undertake the job. I think that was part of his self-confidence.

Carnegie had put the offer out to a lot of different people, but Napoleon Hill was the one who took the bull by the horns and followed through. I think Napoleon saw something in Carnegie, and of course he traveled to see him, as he showed interest in the idea. Napoleon had already been acquainted with Ayers, and I'm sure that affected him. Ayers had been a boy in the Civil War, then he read law, passed the bar, and became successful. By the time that Napoleon met Carnegie, I think he understood that you could do certain things to enhance your chances of success.

That was in 1908. Hill got married shortly after that. He ran an ad for a bride in a Washington paper and ended up marrying a girl from a rich family in West Virginia; her uncle was important in West Virginia government.

Actually, two girls were attending school and living in a boarding house. Napoleon went to see the one that answered the ad, but the other one was coming down the stairs, and he ended up with her. I think it was love at first sight. He didn't marry the one that answered the ad; he married the other one.

One thing that stands out about Hill is that although many people have written about success, he not only wrote about it but gave you the *how*. Whether he's talking about forming a winning personality or applied faith or developing a burning desire, he tells you over and over how to acquire these things, step by step. Even today, I don't think anybody does it better than he did.

Even if you only read the six steps to riches in *Think and Grow Rich*, follow them, and apply them, you're in pretty good shape.

That's where the *how* comes in. You can have all the ingredients that go into a cake and put them all on the table, but you've got to have some basic instruction to get the cake to turn out the way you want. Similarly, besides just having a bunch of material or success stories, you need to know the how, one step at a time. For example, if you develop burning desire but skip the planning part, your results are probably not going to be good.

Hill tells us over and over again: the main thing is making plans and starting. He used to ask his audiences, "How many times on average does a person try something before quitting?" They would say one, three, five, or seven times. He would say, "No, I said on the average." He said that the average is less than one, because most people never start. Some people will make two or three attempts. In Edison's case, he tried ten thousand times before he developed the incandescent light. That's persistence. If you read Steve Jobs's books, the main theme you'll get out of them is persistence.

Even though he died in 1970, I never got the chance to meet Napoleon Hill. Yet in a sense I feel that I have met him, and he has been a mentor to me posthumously.

In early years, we all attribute success to material things. I think I got over it real quick at an early age. It's like that song by Peggy Lee: "Is That All There Is?"

I think I learned this much earlier than Hill, because he bought a Rolls-Royce and an estate and so forth. I can remember my goals at age twenty. I wrote them out on a 3 x 5 card: a million dollars in the bank, a gold Rolex, and a black Mercedes. I showed it to my wife, and she said, "Yes. You're pretty good at doing what you say. I believe you."

I put the card in the top drawer of my nightstand.

She said, "Don't you tell anybody."

"I wasn't going to tell anybody."

"If you do, they'll know you're crazy."

We used to laugh about that. I think it's only normal that at an early age, you dream of acquiring those things. It didn't take me nearly as long as it did Hill to find out that I could make a difference in other people's lives. Money is a tool, that's all. It can buy medication to be sent to St. Jude; it could pay for a kid's college education. The same money can be used for other, destructive items. We do get to choose, and it takes a while for us to mature into that philosophy.

Napoleon Hill came to that conclusion in his life as well. His thinking changed. In his *Master-Key to Riches*, he wrote about the twelve great riches of life, and economic security was only number twelve. He had changed his mind. The last book that was published prior to his death was *Grow Rich with Peace of Mind*. He knew it was a complete myth that money alone will bring happiness. He said, "If you can't find happiness in your work, you'll not be able to find happiness in your life."

Yes, I think he matured. A book published in 1971, a year after he died, was *You've Worked Your Own Miracles*. It was a book of hope, a small book, but Random House published it, and it didn't take long for them to sell a million copies.

I can see where he changed. I think he changed much later than I did. At an early age I was trying to help other people, even though it was on a lot smaller a scale than today. I learned there was a gift from doing these things. You feel good about yourself. You can't feel good about other people if it doesn't start with yourself. I've seen that we've had a positive effect in so many lives. As I told my mom, I can't fix all of them, but with the ones you can, I can make a difference.

In the end, you and I learn the material, and it benefits us, but if we learn the material and we teach it to others, we help others learn. And if we teach others to teach, there really is no limit to where it can go. The effect is absolutely unbelievable, and even today I still enjoy hearing of people who have read a book and been influenced by it. It's still affecting people today. You read stories of Mitt Romney, Billy Ray Cyrus, Steve Harvey, Daymond John, Jim Stovall, Reverend Billy Graham—the list goes on and on and on. I was told that the last time he talked to him, Jim Stovall asked Graham what he'd been reading besides the Bible. He said, "I've been reading *Going the Extra Mile* and *Think and Grow Rich*." It's had a positive effect on lots of people.

Mission Statement

The mission statement of the Napoleon Hill Foundation is to make the world a better place to live in, and how better can we do that than getting his books published in so many places? We have licensed course material in Japan and they've been wonderful friends and unbelievable partners; I've been there three times. They've published every book we've done, I think. It's also important to sell the courses and enable people to teach the material, not just getting the books but actually learning to become instructors. Then they can teach it and explain it to people. This is being done for quite a while now, especially in Japan, Brazil, and other countries. They don't teach so much on a one-on-one basis, but use courses.

A couple of times years ago, I met Dave Liniger, who founded RE/MAX. I believe it's the largest realtor in the United States, maybe the world; I allowed him to use the principles of success, and he put them on a full page in a book he did for his employees. It's a great part of their training.

Then there's the story of Joe Dudley, an unbelievable guy: he founded Dudley Products, the largest minority-owned cosmetic company in the United States. They considered him retarded. He said the saddest day in his life was when he was seventeen and in love. The girl he was going with said, "Joe, I love you, but I'll never be able to marry you."

"Why?" he said.

"I'm afraid our kids will be born retarded."

Joe had a speech impediment, which they mistook for a mental defect. Of course, now old Joe comes to visit me in a chauffeur-driven Cadillac. I wonder if that girl ever wondered what happened to him. He's remarkable, and he's got four or five children who went to MIT and Harvard and other big-name colleges. He started a business in Africa with Nelson Mandela, Cosmetic People, which employed thousands in Africa. When he got the business going and successful, he turned the business over to Mandela. That's the kind of person he is.

Joe says he's read *Think and Grow Rich* three hundred times. When he was having his eighty-fifth birthday, they were having a party for him. He invited me down, but I had a commitment I could not get out of, and I asked a friend to go in my place. He called me and said, "I'm sitting at the table with six billionaires, the richest African-Americans in the United States, who are honoring Joe, and I see a picture of Napoleon Hill hanging here."

Eternal Principles

People sometimes ask me if these principles still apply in the age of current technology. As I see it, certain principles never change. Think of gravity. Say you visit your grandpa on a weekend, and he's got a barn that's seventy-five feet high. You're up in the loft, and you decide to jump off. Gravity is going to cause you to hit the ground. It doesn't matter if you did this last summer or today or five years from now. It's the same thing. You get the same results.

These principles are really old. All Napoleon Hill did was put them together. For example, in Jesus's time, the Jewish people were being made into beasts of burden for the Roman army. They complained, and Jesus said, when a man asks you to go a mile, go two: that means do more than is expected. It's still true when we talk about success today. It's following the principle of doing your job and then some; do what's required and then some. If you have a friend, do more than normally is done, and then some. "And then some" pretty well explains it. It's never changed.

Billy Ray Cyrus learned persistence when he started in the music business. He'd been thrown out of school. He befriended a Dr. Bailey, whose car was broken down on the side of the road. Dr. Bailey was impressed, because he didn't expect a young person to stop and help him. He gave Billy Ray his card and told him to come by his office; he wanted to talk to him, and he did. He gave him *Think and Grow Rich*.

Billy Ray said he read that book and got to the point about persistence. He said it was as if a voice had spoken to him and said, "Billy Ray, buy yourself a guitar and start your band." He bought one, and he remembered that persistence theme from *Think and Grow Rich*. He said that on some nights, they would get $50 or $100; they played beer joints, rough places, where there were fights. He stuck with it. After a number of years, he came out with that song "Achy Breaky Heart" that girls like to dance to.

Of course, Billy Ray also tells the story of his daughter Miley. He called her Smiley. He said she could sing when she was three years old. When she went to show business, they dropped the S, and she became Miley.

Entertainer Steve Harvey says he's read *Think and Grow Rich* twenty-five times. He was homeless at one time—just a tremendous story. Everybody's got a story. That's how we learn.

It's absolutely amazing, because it works. There are no magic wands, but there are certain things that successful people do that other people either don't know or are not willing to do. It all starts inside of us. What we are on the outside is simply a reflection or what we are on the inside. Both poverty and riches reflect what we are on the inside.

TWO

Some Ideas on Success

I have a few basic personal principles for success:

1. Have a desire to improve.
2. Belief is a state of mind.
3. Believe you can accomplish your purpose in life.
4. Feedback is what you get for taking action.
5. Repetition means doing the action over and over until it becomes a habit.

The formula in my book *Everything I Know about Success I Learned from Napoleon Hill* is gleaned from my own experience as well as Hill's. Basically I've rewritten the old *Think and*

Grow Rich. On the first page is the question, what do you want? That's the starting point. What do you want? Why? What do you desire? You have to start somewhere or another. Although things may change as you go along, at least you're starting on a road.

Think of things that you want to accomplish. Personally, I think you have to write them down. I can remember giving a talk once at the Chamber of Commerce in which I talked about goal setting. At the break, a schoolteacher came up to me and said, "I always make goals," but, she added, "I don't write them down."

"That's what we call dreams," I said.

When you decide what you want and write it down, you look at it as a contract with yourself: "This is what I am going to do." You make all the plans for what you want, but you also have to do something about it.

Goals in Your Pocket

It's easy to have goals in your pocket. You have a moment at the red light, or you're waiting for someone at lunch. You pull out the card, and you've got three or four goals. You look at the card and say, "Gosh, this is July; I haven't done anything on that. I've let several months go by."

You keep your written goals in front of you. I'm not saying that people can't do it in their minds, but I think it's good to refresh the memory.

Borrowing a little from my good friend Dr. Denis Waitley, I've said to clients and colleagues, "Go home, look at the calendar and hunt for Someday." I said, "Someday is the biggest lie we've ever told in our life. Someday I'm going to die. Someday I'm going to go visit my relatives or see my mom, or someday I'm going to start a book, or someday I'll pay off my credit card, or someday I'm going to start investing." It's plain that we have lied to ourselves.

We have to make a commitment, and I've learned that you don't always meet your goals when you think you will. It may take longer than you planned, but that doesn't mean you've failed.

I'll give you an example. When I was in banking, I thought it was worthwhile to put up a historical marker for Napoleon Hill. All throughout the State of Virginia, you've got signs saying that George Washington slept here and crossed the river here, markers for Civil War battles and similar things. I wrote a letter saying I would like to put a Napoleon Hill marker up. They wrote me back and said, "To start off with, the person would have to be dead for fifty years." Hill had only been dead for around twenty years.

Was I supposed to quit? I didn't take no for an answer. I found the Virginia Historical Society, who are the ones responsible for maintaining and putting up those markers. I got the list of directors. When I had a break, I would call one of them. They would say, "Oh, we'll take a look at it"; basically, they pushed me off. There were a dozen or so on the board, and I probably called five or six of them. I finally got a guy from Culpeper, Virginia. I remember that he worked as a court clerk. I told him what I was trying to do, and he said, "Man, I think that's wonderful. I read that book. It's made all the difference in the world to me." He said, "You don't have to do anything else. I'll take it from here."

I kept up with him. Of course, I went through all the politicians, the congressmen, senators, everybody I could contact, to get some leverage. The board met three or four times a year. Several months went by, and I got a letter saying they probably could do it, but at this point, they had no money left in the budget for that fiscal year.

I got back in touch with the director I knew and said, "That's fine. I'll pay for it." Now what kind of excuse could he come up with? I think it was around $1,100. It was no big deal. I gave them the information to put on the marker. The whole process took me longer than I expected—it happened more than a year later than I said I'd get it done.

For the opening, I invited Hill's family and the media. It was a tremendous gathering; people were lining the sides of the highway. The board couldn't believe it. "We never had a turnout like this," they said.

"Well," I said, "you've never put a marker up for Napoleon Hill before." The marker is still maintained today.

Persistence makes all the difference between success and mediocrity. Everybody has ideas, but it's what you do with the them that counts. Ideas themselves are worthless until they are put into place. You can have the best idea in the world, but only you can say when you will go and do something about it. Yes, it may be more difficult than you thought. It may take more planning, and you may have to change your plans. You may need help. We call upon the Master Mind: we get other people to help us.

If we have the idea, we find the way to accomplish it. That's the important thing. It separates the people who are successful from failures and mediocrities. The latter simply don't plan, or their plans are weak, or they don't persist in what they're working on.

You Are Responsible

Let me look a little more deeply into this statement: "The power to be what you want to be and get what you desire resides in you. You are responsible."

A challenge to this philosophy that's very prevalent in our society today is that we *aren't* responsible; our identity limits our opportunities. The restrictions come from a variety of things, from how we look to gender, class, and all sorts of things. We are also affected by systemic issues in our economy and our society.

I would reply by saying you have to accept responsibility for yourself—self-reliance. I don't care if somebody is born illegitimate or on the wrong side of the tracks. We have a social environment in which we grow up. It's true that there are some things we can't change, such as our physical environment. We have a lot of restrictions on us, but we also have a lot of things we can do to shape who we are.

For example, we can stay away from negative people. As Mark Twain said, "Don't walk away, run from them, because they do have an influence on you." Every person that we meet has an influence on us. So does every book we read. Of course, we have to choose whether that influence will be positive or negative. In the final analysis, it rests with us. It might take a lot of willpower to accept that responsibility, but you will never be a tremendous success unless you do. There is a saying: "If it is to be, it's up to me."

It's really easy to say, "I didn't go to the right school" and such things. You can have a list a mile long, but it won't get you anywhere. You'll find a new day when you start saying, "I'm responsible. This is what I'm going to do, even though I don't know how I'm going to get there."

We always know something. We don't have all the answers, but we have to have faith that we can start out and find the right stops and the right turns. When you're traveling, you don't go back home if there are roads under construction or a highway is closed. You simply go back and find another route until you get there.

I think it all begins with accepting responsibility. You can start off making excuses, but you'll just find it that much easier to make another excuse, and another. It takes some grit, but the problems we solve strengthen us. Every time we solve a problem—and we are going to have problems—it makes us more resilient and more self-reliant, because we'll have gone through it or something similar to it before. Even though we didn't know the answers, we got them, so why can't we do it again? With anything that we can do well, the more we do it, the more we repeat it, the better we get.

When I discuss a book, people will say, "I read that book a long time ago; why should I read it again?"

I tell them, "Hey, you're smarter than I am. I didn't get my ABCs the first time. I also had to say the multiplication tables over and over."

If we do something enough, it can be embedded in our subconscious until it becomes a part of us. The same is true with the negatives: "This won't work. My wife told me it wouldn't. I don't know why we started." If you develop that attitude, you will not have great accomplishments.

Often the greater the difficulty, the more opportunity there is, because the world's full of opportunities whether you see them or not. If there's a problem, somebody is going to solve it one way or the other, and they're going to benefit from it.

Wealth and the Desire for Wealth

There is another principle: "To obtain wealth, you must have the desire for wealth."

Some people ask how you can develop this to the level of a burning desire if you don't have it.

Some people have more of a burning desire because they come from a disadvantaged background, but it's not necessarily so. Take Bill Gates: he was raised in an upper-middle-class family, but he developed his principles out of a desire to accomplish something worthwhile. It's not all about the money, although the bigger the project is, the more likely it is that you'll make money.

Of course, money should never be a goal in itself. It's the use of money and what you can accomplish with it in the world. I could show you the first edition of *Think and Grow Rich*. At the top of the cover, it said, "For men and women who resent poverty." Hill wrote it for the millions of men and women who were living in poverty and fear of poverty.

Some people find poverty easy to accept. I read a story years ago about a man and his neighbor out in the country. They were sitting on the porch, talking. The man lived in a rough, unpainted house. He had a big dog, and it was lying there. The dog would moan and make sounds. The visitor asked the man, "What's wrong with your dog?"

"That board he's lying on has a nail in it. It's sticking up."

"Why don't he just get up and move?"

"He's not hurting that bad."

I think this story explains a lot about accomplishment. There's nothing wrong with being satisfied with mediocrity, but if you have a burning desire for something, you're going to have to take certain steps to accomplish it.

People have many different motives for getting money. Somebody may want a better lifestyle and security, or they may want to help certain causes—medicine, church, education, anything to make the world a better place. For each one of us, it's got to be developed within. Somebody can't walk up to you and say, "I want you to get this burning desire to get this accomplished."

Some people are going to have more burning desire and persistence than others, but the degree to which they have it will have a direct relation to what they accomplish in life.

The same principle can be applied to other things in life, because whether you're writing your next book or improving a community or organizing a Little League baseball team, you're going to have to take the same steps. You have to have a burning desire, a plan, and persistence in following the steps to accomplishing what you want.

Believe in Yourself

Another part of the formula is to believe in yourself. The only limitations are those you place on yourself.

You may ask how realistic that is and how you distinguish a healthy belief in yourself from self-delusion. How do you separate what's realistic from what's unrealistic when it comes to believing in yourself?

To begin with, I would say that you have to be careful about being too willing to accept what cannot be done. Physical limitations do exist: a guy who's blind probably cannot become a good sharpshooter. Nonetheless, I think we can be too ready to accept such beliefs as, "I'm too old to start now," "I don't have the money to start with," or "We're not living in the right community." These are the people Hill said never even start. They may have an idea, but if they don't make some plans and actually begin, it's not likely to be realized.

Even if you have some physical limitations that might disqualify you for a certain career, your ability is usually far beyond what you think it is. Don't be too quick to discount yourself.

My good friend Jim Stovall has been blind since college. You might think that a blind person can't write a book, but this guy's done over forty books. He's read ten times as many books through audiobooks as I have. One of his books sold five million copies and was made into a movie that grossed over $100 million. He had to go about it in a different manner, but he did not accept defeat.

At one point, Jim was in his room and thought he'd be there for the rest of his life. One day the idea hit him to go check the mailbox. He couldn't read, but he wondered if he could make it to the mailbox. He made it to the mailbox and made it back. This idea came to him: "Every road leads anywhere in the world you want to go."

In about six months, he was speaking in Madison Square Garden in front of thousands of people. He's one of the most highly paid speakers out there today.

We can be too easy to discount ourselves and make excuses like, "I don't know the right people" or "I don't have the capital to start with." Napoleon Hill said that only after he started did he learn that you need $100,000 to start a successful magazine.

He didn't know that beforehand. It was a tremendous success, and it was started with no money.

We've got to be careful about taking the easy way out. It's about commitment to something you really desire because you think it's the only way you can feel fulfilled. None of us reach our potential, but you can use more of your potential than you can by doing nothing.

Optimism versus Delusion

Of course you have to separate optimism from delusion. I think optimism is simply having a belief that you can accomplish something. Delusion would be, when you're on top of a ten-story building, believing you could jump off and it wouldn't hurt you. By contrast, an optimist might say that if you want to go from the tenth floor to the ground, you could simply take the elevator or do something else that's feasible.

Delusion is fooling yourself, not dealing with reality. Although the statement is, "Our only limitations are the ones we set in our own mind," we do have to take some limitations into account. If you think you can jump off of the Empire State Building and not get hurt, you're delusional. There's a difference between being a realistic optimist and being unrealistic, with a feeling that you could jump off a bridge without hurting yourself.

Motivational speaker Jim Rohn said, "It's not what happens to you. It's what you do about what happens." It's really easy to develop a belief such as, "I'm the only person who ever got laid off. I'm the only person who ever had cancer."

I think we get better as we go along; it's what we call experience. People sometimes ask, why read a book more than once? Of course, you learn by repeating, but you're also a different person the second time around. If you first read a good book twenty years ago and you read it today, not a word in the book will have changed, it's the same material, but our interpretation of it will be different because of other books we've read and conversations we've had. Our outlook has changed. It's like the man who said that when he was fifteen, he knew without a doubt that his dad was the most stupid person on earth. By the time he got to thirty, he said, "It was amazing how much the old man had learned."

It's easy to discount that fact, but we do change. Hopefully we do, because life is a long-term learning process. If we think we know it all, we're in bad shape, because the more you learn, the more you realize what you don't know. There's a lot out there from which we can keep learning if we so desire.

As I've said, we learn by two means: from books and from other people. Hopefully, we're always going to be around people that are a lot smarter than we are. The best way to learn is to associate with people who are smarter than you.

It's said that dominant thoughts make your inner world. Given the importance of this principle, you need to make sure that healthy, goal-oriented thoughts are your dominant thoughts. It can be tricky. If someone says, "Don't think of a pink elephant," a pink elephant will be all you can think of. Sometimes when people are going through a negative time or there's a lot of negativity around them, it can be hard to change their stream of thoughts.

The one item that will remove negative thoughts is action: doing something else. I remember there used to be a little spot on TV featuring a lady from the mountains of Erwin, Tennessee, who was up in years. She said, "When I get too worried about things, I come out here and hoe my garden, because I can't hoe and worry at the same time." She replaced her words with action.

A lot of people think that vision boards are silly, but they work. A vision board is a collection of pictures or words showing things you want to become. You put it in a place where you will see it frequently. It's a constant reminder of what you want. One guy got a picture of a guy in BVD shorts and put it up in his bathroom, where he could see it every day, in order to motivate him to lose weight.

In 1975, the year I started the bank, I could not find a house I could afford. I bought a townhouse, but my wife really wasn't satisfied with it, because we had had a house in Tennessee that we built, which I had leased to a doctor. We wanted something comparable to what we had.

One day my wife was looking at an issue of *Better Homes and Gardens*. It had an ad that showed a picture of a two-story house made out of cedar. They just used it in the ad because it was a pretty picture. My wife said, "That's really something."

I said, "You like this?"

"Yes, because it's got two porches on it. You can go from the master bedroom out onto one porch. Then there's a porch when you come in." The house also had a long den and a couple of fireplaces, one in the den and one in the master bedroom. We really liked it, but it was just a picture.

I wrote to the company that placed the ad and asked them about the house. They wrote back and said that it was in Brander-mill, Virginia, which is outside of Richmond.

So be it. I took the picture and put it up inside a closet door so that every time I got out towels or took a bath, I would see that picture. A few weeks later, the CEO of the bank asked me to attend a conference of the Federal Reserve in Richmond. I asked my wife to go. I said, "We'll stop and look at that house on the way back."

We did. It was in a housing development. The guy that built it wasn't there, but they had salespeople on hand. I got his name and address, and when we got back, I ordered a set of the plans. We looked at it further; then I got someone to build that house.

I built that house in 1976, and I still live in it. It all started out from a picture or a vision board, but I could see that house, and my wife could too.

It's amazing how things seem to fall in place once we concentrate, because as we know, it all begins in the thought process. Nothing was done without beginning in thought. Pictures remind us of what we want or want to accomplish in life, and it becomes a part of our subconscious.

A Strong Purpose

The next principle is to have a strong, well-ascertained purpose in life. Lately—maybe because we're spending so much time with our digital selves, where we're not as connected physically as we used to be—people seem to be losing that sense of purpose, the sense of "I'm here for a reason. I'm doing something productive that I want to do and that serves people." Yet a sense of purpose is extremely important, because without it we become aimless drifters, like tumbleweeds.

Today a lack of self-confidence is overwhelming among youth. They don't feel that they have a great purpose. They can get in trouble, because they don't have something in front of them for which they've really developed a desire. That's why they have a strong desire to fit in.

Of course, nobody can assign them a purpose; they have to do it on their own. But it needs to be brought to their attention that they really need to decide.

Sometimes you ask a man what his son is doing, and he says, "He's trying to find himself."

This is fine if you're college age, but at some time or another, you need to decide on something that makes you want to get up in the morning. If you want to be successful, you have a purpose that you think about when you're going to bed, when you wake up, and when you have lunch. If you do, it'll turn out— maybe not as quickly or well as you want—but you'll be amazed at the results.

Norman Vincent Peale once gave a lecture on the topic that every problem has a solution. He started off by telling about a lady who climbed up on a steeple in England and threatened to jump. A crowd gathered, and they got a policeman to talk to her. It didn't work; she still said she was going to jump. The crowd got bigger. They finally sent for a minister. He talked to her, but that didn't work either. She jumped and took her life. Dr. Peale said, "The minister did not know what problem that woman had. No matter what her problem was, it had a solution to it."

Some people become successful just out of necessity.

Someone might not have that much desire for money, but they will have a fulfilled life if they find a purpose and fulfill it. It's the same with work. If you can't find something that you can happily spend your hours at, you're going to have a miserable existence. You'll hate to go to work on Mondays.

In the end it's your own responsibility. I can't tell you what you lack. Some answers you have to find yourself. But if we don't try to get those answers, we'll be leading a miserable life, because somebody else can't find our purpose for us.

My brother's granddaughter Alexis wanted to go to veterinary school. Not only does she love animals, but she's prepared herself in school. She's a straight A student, and she's graduating from Mississippi State University. Getting into a veterinary school is not easy, but she has a desire to accomplish something, and she's had her mind on it. Now, Alexis has been accepted in the veterinary program at Lincoln Memorial University.

You can't just wake up one morning and say, "I want to be a vet" or "I want to be a banker." You have to do some home-work, and again it comes down to developing a purpose in your life and deciding what you want. A lot of people go all the way through life and never have a purpose. This takes us away from our self-responsibility and self-reliance, because when we're allowed to do something on our own, we have liberty. When we let somebody else do it for us, it's tyranny.

If you live in Chicago and say, "I hate these cold winters," quit talking about it. Get up and move. You can solve the prob-lem if you want to, but some people would rather complain than change their circumstances because it's become their habit to make excuses. You may think that complaining absolves you of responsibility, but it doesn't get you anywhere. It won't have a positive outcome.

Determine Your Goals

Another principle of the formula for success is "Determine your goals and plans and get started. A task, once begun, is half done." Some people wonder what they should focus on in their goals and plans.

I think it goes back to childhood and what we enjoy doing. For a lot of people, the dream dies in them if they don't cultivate it, take care of it, or do something about it. As children, we may dream of becoming a professional athlete or a banker or a vet-erinarian. We cultivate this dream by doing things that move us closer to it. For example, if you're going to work at a job that requires a lot of education, you can't ignore this fact. You've got to start at an early age and find out, "Hey, I have to take chemistry; I have to take biology." It's just a series of steps. Each one takes us a little closer.

What drove you when you were a kid? You can read about the astronauts. From a very early age, they admired planes and flying. They didn't wake up one day and say, "I will be an astronaut." There was a lot of requirements they had to meet.

I think it's important to go back to your childhood—maybe not your childhood dream as such, but something for which you can have a passion. Something that will get you up, draw you, and become both a passion and a belief system. Then you can accomplish your goal.

We start by making plans and taking steps—but we start. It's never too early or too late to start. You start, and you move one step at a time with belief, because without that, you probably won't start or take the necessary steps. You'll develop the belief that it's just not working and abandon your dreams. One way or another, you have to set your sights on something—"This is what I'm going to do"—and take one step at a time with persistence and a belief that you can accomplish it.

As I've said, I write down goals on an index card. Actually putting them down on paper is important for the process rather than just holding that idea in your head. I look at it as a contract with myself and a constant reminder, saying, "This is what I'm going to do." You can use a vision board or an index card if you want, but stick that thing where you see it over and over again. I can pull my drawer open at work and look at goals that I've written down.

Try to do something about your goal on a regular basis, and move it up one step at a time. When we were growing up, they told us to focus on one thing and do it well, but you have to be realistic. If I've written a book and my agent is out there pitching it, it may take six months to get a good contract. I'm not supposed to do anything else till I get an answer back? In the meantime, I've got to develop other projects and other goals, moving them up one step at a time until they're completed.

Passion: The Missing Ingredient

The next principle in the formula is this: Hard work and integrity are necessary, but not enough. Passion is the missing ingredient.

You may say that passion—or at least passionate displays of emotion—are all over the place in our society, especially on social media, while workers who have integrity and a strong work ethic are in shorter supply. Yet even those things—honesty and hard work—are not enough for success.

It takes more than just being honest. In life, you have to apply yourself. Then you have the rewards for doing things no one else is doing. People who do something a little better and a little more responsibly are going to be rewarded in proportion to what they put into it.

Honesty is integrity. Lots of people out there are trying to show success by displays of wealth. To me, success is the way other people see you. You don't have to do anything except lead your life being honest and helping as many as you can of your choosing. Recognition is earned and not bought.

You can buy all kinds of recognition today. You can go give a donation to some institution, and they'll give you an honorary doctorate. Or you can go on the Internet and order one. Somebody, I never found out who, sent me a certificate that made me a minister of some church. Probably they paid a few bucks for it. This is funny, because we earn our reputation; we don't buy it.

Again, I think it's important to do something you really love. For example, people love to fish. Some people just want it as a hobby; others take it and make a living with it. There's good money in making fishing lures.

I've got a first cousin who got to making knives—big knives—and he's been at it probably more than forty years. It's a painstaking process, but you're talking about $2,500 or more for a knife.

Of course it started out as a hobby, but he loved doing it. He worked, but he also developed the hobby until it overtook his job. It started out that way, but he loves what he's doing. He sells his knives at shows. I actually went to a couple that were close by. I can't imagine somebody paying $2,500 or more for a knife that's never going to be used, but people have different desires.

In any case, my cousin took a hobby that he loved and made it into a profession. I think that's where the passion comes in.

You'll get good at something if you apply yourself, correct your mistakes, practice, and get feedback. At the least you'll be a lot better than average.

Getting and Giving Help

The last main part of this formula is: Get others to help you make progress, and give to others. It's almost a matter of doing nothing but attracting people that enjoy working with you.

One example is my book *Three Feet from Gold*, which I completed with the help of Sharon Lechter. At one point, my late friend Charlie "Tremendous" Jones, who ran Executive Books, introduced me to a young man named Greg Reid. He said, "Greg's gone through some struggles. Do you think you could get a writing job for him?"

At the time I had the vision for *Three Feet from Gold*. I told Greg to see what he could do with it. He got up to eighty pages, and he got some appointments for us in New York. A literary agent took us to the Waldorf Astoria, and we met different people, but the project never went anywhere.

Sharon Lechter had contacted me before about writing something. She was deeply moved by *Think and Grow Rich* when she was in college. She's a CPA, but she's coauthored fourteen books with Robert Kiyosaki that have sold 37 million copies, although they dissolved their partnership. I told her about my book. We went to New York and pitched it to Leonard Riggio, founder of Barnes and Nobles, and his PR people. They made a best seller initiative out of it, and it hit the best seller list right off the bat.

It was an amazing project, and we're publishing the tenth anniversary edition. It's sold extremely well in foreign countries also, because it's a story of persistence. In any case, it's amazing how little I did. I had an idea, but I certainly did not make it a success.

I think it's the same at work. If you're not worried about who's getting credit, you'll do well. I've always taken that position: I've never asked for a raise in my life, and I've never asked for a job, although people are always recruiting me.

If you're worried about egos or getting your name on something, you can't expect maximum results. Give people credit, and it'll be amazing what you can accomplish and how they will enjoy working with you. We want to promote them; we want to help them. It's amazing what people will do for you when you call on them.

You've got to get help from other people. If you try to do everything yourself, you're not going to get much done. You need to continually reach out to people in the business who can help you. Give them an idea, and see what they can do with it.

Napoleon Hill defined success as getting anything you want in life without detriment to other people. Each person has to define their own success. A little sign on my desk says, "Success is a journey, not a destination," which simply means that it's not just saying, "I've got to get a gold Rolex, a black Mercedes, and a million bucks to make me a success, and that's it."

It's the type of person that we become, because we change. We see new ways of helping people, making a difference, and giving assistance to others. The road to success is more than just saying, "Look at my bank balance or my stock portfolio." It's the type of person that we've grown into during the process.

In the beginning, Napoleon Hill was more concerned with material things. I think it took him longer than most of us would to realize that it's about making a difference rather than just looking out for ourselves. His motivation changed, as you can see in *The Master-Key to Riches*, which is about attaining peace of mind. We mature, we grow better, we grow bigger. Again, that's left up to each one of us individually.

A lot of people, especially the younger ones, define success in terms of money. OK. We won't mention names, but we know a famous boxer who made several hundred million dollars. He ended up in jail, and he ended up bankrupt. He made all that money, but would you consider him a success? The local drug dealer, who drives a Lamborghini and has gold chains around his neck and girls hanging on, made his money selling opioids. Would you consider him a success?

Money may indicate that you did something successfully, but it doesn't make you a success. It's the good you do with what you make and the fact that you made it honestly, without hurting other people. As Hill said, it's getting what you want in life without doing harm to other people.

I'll say it simply: you can have your money, or your money can have you. When your money has you, you're in trouble, because you're trying to impress people; you're trying to buy fancy cars or other signs of wealth.

I have friends that are worth millions and millions, but they're polite, they're generous. I can remember one of them in particular. He's in the coal business. At a restaurant, I would always see him eating in an out-of-the-way location; you would never know he was there. If he left before I did, he would always come by the table and speak, but he wasn't seeking anything. He would not try to draw attention to himself. Another one of my mentors is Jim Brown. In the early days, he bought Rolls-Royces, but the last time I was with him, he was driving a Ford SUV.

I think it's natural for a lot of people to display wealth when they're young. Some learn the lesson more quickly than others, and maybe some never do. They spend a lot of money trying to buy a reputation or displaying showmanship: "Stand here and look at me."

We often speak of leaving a legacy. That's a misnomer, because I think a better term is "living a legacy." See some of the things you've accomplished while you're still here; enjoy the success stories of kids growing up and becoming doctors or pharmacists or CPAs. I think it's much more fulfilling to see things that you've done to benefit others while you're still here. Why do you have to wait to die before you leave something?

Don't just leave a legacy; live a legacy.

THREE

Adversity and Failure

*You gain strength, courage and confidence by every
experience in which you really stopped to look fear in the
face. You are able to say to yourself, "I have lived through
this horror. I can take the next thing that comes along."
You must do the thing you think you cannot do.*
—ELEANOR ROOSEVELT

I have used this quote in some of my writings about adversity
and failure. Why is it so powerful?

We can accept a setback either as a defeat or as a lesson. I've
got all kinds of examples. The first one that pops into my mind
has to do with art. At the beginning, I just studied it, but when I
got to banking, I starting buying some art.

I met a man, whom I will call Dr. Nikita. He came over as an exchange professor from Moscow University, and I met him through the college system. His stepfather, he told me, was a famous painter named Eugene Kumanov. He designed the set for the movie *War and Peace*. I knew of him, but I didn't know his paintings. It led to me buying a lot of Russian art.

I also began selling art at auction, and I'd always done well. At one point I sent eight or nine paintings to an auction house called Sloans & Kenyon. The auction was in Bethesda, Maryland, and the people attending were all rich Russians living in the suburbs of Washington, D.C. It was a nice event, with cheese and wine. Then they started selling my paintings, but they didn't bring what I thought they ought to bring. I thought I would see them sell for three, four, or five times what I paid for them, but they didn't. Two or three of them lost money.

I didn't need the money, but I thought it was kind of funny. Later I realized that all I needed to do was put a minimum on the price: if it didn't sell at or above the minimum, I kept the painting—but I didn't put that in the contract.

I didn't quit selling art. Since then, when I've had a painting auctioned off, I've said, "This has got to bring $5,000, or I don't sell," and put that in the contract. I learned from that experience, although I could have taken it as a failure. We can take failures as lessons, or we can let them defeat us. We're only failures when we quit trying, when we don't learn something and keep trying. The amount of money it cost me was well worth the lesson I learned.

Conquest Brings Strength

I think that's what Eleanor Roosevelt was talking about. Each time we conquer something, it gives us strength. It gives us resilience for the next event. If something else comes up, we can say, "This is like what happened before." There's a lesson learned, and we can go on to something else.

Things are not going to go right for us every day. We can take them as part of the learning process, because you will never swim across the river if you don't get in the water. You've got to start and do the best you can with what you've got in front of you, but with a belief that the results are going to be good. It may not always be, but at least you have that belief, and you protect yourself as well as you can. You've got to be doing something; you've got to be active.

There's nobody out there who hasn't been affected by adversities. My friend Jim Stovall is blind, but he doesn't consider himself handicapped. How could he? He authored one book that was made into a movie and grossed $100 million. He has wrote forty-seven books and was named one of the ten most noted persons in the world in the same year as Mother Teresa.

Jim would probably never have developed as he did if he still had his sight, because he had to stop playing professional football. At age twenty, he went for a physical and discovered he had macular degeneration. He was going blind. He says there's not a lot of blind players in the NFL—a few blind referees maybe, but no players. It's a tremendous story, because he had every right in the world to just stay home and sit there.

Victor Frankl's *Man's Search for Meaning* describes how the author dealt with the horror of Auschwitz. It's an amazing story, and I can't even fathom what happened to him. He discovered that he had control over only one thing, which was his mind. They could do anything they wanted to with him. They could put him to death. He survived because he was in control of his mind, his thought process. He looked forward to finishing his work; he looked forward to seeing his family. Unfortunately, all of his family were put to death, but that's what drove him: he had a reason to live. Over and over he said, "That's the one thing that separates us from animals: we have control over our mind." We may not utilize it, but we have control over our mind.

They could do anything they wanted to, but they couldn't change his thought process. With his drive, he did little things, like using a piece of glass to keep his beard as close-shaven as he could, so he didn't look as old. He was careful to make sure not to limp or do anything that might get him gassed. On some days, if somebody had been caught trying to escape, they wouldn't feed him. He got potatoes and buried them where he could find them. On the days that they had no food, he would scrape the dirt off and eat them. It kept him going.

It's amazing what people will do. If they have a *why*, they'll find the *how*. This takes us back to our goals. Why do we want to be a medical doctor? Do we dream of going to Africa to help underdeveloped nations? Why do we want to become what we want to become? When the *why* is strong enough, we'll discover the *how*. It may take us some time; it may take a lot of time. We may have to get help from other people. But if we know why we want to do something and it's strong enough, we'll find a how.

The Setbacks of Napoleon Hill

Napoleon Hill himself suffered many setbacks during his career, because he didn't have a knack for money, but he always had the resiliency to come back. In 1919–23, when he was doing his magazines, *Hill's Golden Rule Magazine* and *Napoleon Hill's Magazine*, he had bad business dealings with a partner and lost them.

Hill was probably overoptimistic, but that may also have been a product of the times. For example, after he published *Law of Success* in 1928, he was getting $2,000 and $3,000 a month in royalties. That was a lot of money, but that's when he bought a Rolls-Royce and a 600-acre estate in the Catskill Mountains.

Of course, we know what happened in October 1929: the stock market collapsed. No one was buying anything. I guess he was a victim of circumstances, but even during World War II, he was selling courses, speaking all over the country, and had a lot of enrollments. Of course, young people, whom the courses were meant to appeal to, had gone off to war. They weren't going to be taking lessons or sending money in.

Hill married his first real love in 1910, and this marriage lasted twenty-five years. Then he married Rosa Lee Beeland, who was around twenty-five years younger. She was very good-looking and worked as a secretary. He met her in Atlanta, Georgia and it was love at first sight, or as he said, "I was smitten." She was looking for a man who had a lot of money, which he didn't have, but she contributed a lot. She helped him write *Think and Grow Rich*, for example the chapters on the mystery of sex transmutation. They bought a big mansion down in Florida. Of course, they ended up divorcing; she married her lawyer, I think. That was in the late thirties. When they divorced, she really took him to the cleaners.

Hill had three sons. One of them, David, was one of West Virginia's most decorated soldiers. He served thirty years in the Marines in World War II and the Korean War. One of David's daughters had four sons: three doctors and one banker.

Hill's life turned around in 1941, when he met Annie Lou Norman, his last wife. He was married to her for twenty-seven years, from 1943 till his death in 1970. She was a student in a class he was teaching at a Presbyterian college in Clinton, South Carolina. In fact, he inscribed a book for her: "To my student, Annie Lou Norman." On December 23, 1943, the day they got married, he wrote again in the book, saying, "You had the book, and now you have the author."

He had pretty smooth sailing from then on. Annie Lou was a tremendous help. She had been a bookkeeper, and she kept his finances straight; she also helped to manage bookings. He spoke in eighty different towns in one year. He traveled by car, and he kept ledgers showing that he had, for example, bought $2 worth of gas, paid $3.10 for a meal. Annie Lou typed a lot of his speeches, and she kept his newspaper clippings and speeches from all over the country.

In 1945, Hill wrote *The Master-Key to Riches*. In the back of it, he wrote, "If the reader will send the author a self-addressed stamped envelope, I will send you an autographed bookplate and an essay." He did this to develop a mailing list in order to sell other materials of his.

We still get one or two of these requests every week.

We reprinted the bookplate, and we keep the essays in print. He wrote an essay on tolerance and another on ten rules for success. We printed them up with a border so they are frameable, and people still ask for them. It's a pretty good way of making contact, because I can always stick something in about a new book that has come out or some other product. He did this as a marketing piece, and it's still a good idea.

Keeping on Track

Sometimes it seems that things are almost conspiring to take us off track in our career. Certain forces in the world can pull us away from our goals, our plans, and taking action. We have smartphones, social media, email. In some industries, people get as many as two hundred emails a day. People sometimes ask what advice Hill, who wrote during a very different age, might give us here. For me, it's about separating the important from the unimportant. For example, going in one morning, I may find that my assistant has printed out an unbelievable number of emails. I go through them quickly to see which ones have to do with publications. I rank the things that need to be done, such as a contract with a foreign publisher that our lawyer may have prepared. I'll look it over, sign it, walk it out front, and give it to Zane. He'll scan it and send it to the foreign publisher. Those are pretty routine things, but nothing happens until I get these contracts signed and sent out.

Of course, we get lots of inquiries about Hill: Did he die broke? How many times was he married? Did he sell his typewriter for $10? You could call it the nonsense of people's curiosity. I might get around to answering, but it's certainly no priority. We also get regular requests from prisoners for books. Usually I just hand them to Zane and say, "Send them a book." You can't let those things be priorities. It would not be good to reach the end of the day and find a contract that may be worth several thousand dollars still on my desk.

Separating the important from the unimportant, I may make mistakes. I may choose the wrong thing, it doesn't materialize into anything, but when I first read it, it seemed to be the one that most needed my attention.

With some projects, we're moving a step forward. I constantly have other ones that I have to place on the back burner. It's not always a question of money, because some of the projects that give the most satisfaction pay the least, such as publishing books in Iran and Saudi Arabia.

When I was in finance, I knew I was young, but I felt I could do anything the manager did. I learned credit decisions, and I'd actually been out on the road, and I had seen what problems people confronted. In doing collections, I learned to talk to people, and I learned something. Most people think that collections involve a big guy like a bouncer who goes out and scares the hell out of them so that they cough up and pay.

That might work for a little bit, but people build up resistance. They simply don't open the door. You know there's somebody in there; you hear the radio, and all of a sudden it gets quiet and nobody comes to the door. You may have driven forty or fifty miles or longer to see them, but you can't do anything about it; you can't knock a door down.

Instead, when I talked to them, I would say, "We've got a problem." If they said, "What do you mean, we?" I would say, "Well, the office you owe money to came to me. This is my job. I'm getting paid to get the cash, and I would like to work with you." I sold them on the idea that I was on their side. I would say such things as, "Can you get a payment today; can you borrow from something or another? I've got to go on to Clintwood; I can come back by here." I would try to work with them. I'd say, "You have three payments. If I take one payment back to them, they'll let you keep your car; otherwise they told me to come here and pick up the car, but I don't want to do that. If we do that, we've lost you as a customer. You've been with us, and we'd like to work with you and solve your problem." I learned to appeal to them by being on their side. It was us against the big guys.

Overcoming Fear

In those days, I never traveled far other than taking a car vacation to a national park, such as the Smoky Mountains. I'd fish in a lake and sleep out on the ground, not staying in a room. We lived a very simple life.

I wanted to get promoted badly, and that meant that I had to transfer to Indianapolis. They sent me plane tickets to go to Louisville to be interviewed by the president of the company. I'd never flown, and I was scared to death to fly on a plane. I'd never been to a place as big as Louisville, and to get a taxi to downtown, check in to a hotel, and go to his office was a big challenge, but I wanted the job badly enough to do it.

Then we moved to Indiana. I can recall the first place they put me in—gosh, it was a dump. My wife wasn't with me. I had gone a few weeks early to get situated. It was heartbreaking to her to see the place they moved us into, so I immediately found a duplex in the little town of Mooresville, where John Dillinger was from. All of this was traumatic, but I wanted the job badly enough to overcome it. My desire to succeed caused me to overcome any reluctance or fear that I had.

I could have stayed at my old job, and in a few years, one of the other guys may have retired or died or taken another job, but I could see that there was very little activity. The older guys had been around quite a while. I'd got to meet all of them at meetings, and none of them was really up in years. They were probably in their forties, fifties, and sixties. I was extremely ambitious. I couldn't wait to get promoted. I didn't think I was that much smarter, but I was willing to work harder than most of the people I was around. If there is a secret, that's it—going the extra mile, and then some. In any case, the desire to get ahead outweighed anything that was holding me back.

Before my wife, to whom I'd been married for fifty-four years, passed away, she told my daughter Donna, "Don't ever let your daddy quit work. He wouldn't live fifteen minutes."

At the time of this writing, I'm seventy-nine. Trustees ask me, "Don, how long are you going to work?" I'll say, "As long as I have the feelings and the passion I have right now, I don't see an end in sight." I've never set a goal like retiring at sixty-five or seventy. Retire to what? I've got the best life on earth. Why would I want to quit? It doesn't make sense. There are other things I want to do in addition, such as working with the University of Virginia, but I can do those too. There are constantly things that I can do to make a contribution. I still get a thrill out of seeing them happen. Some of them don't happen to the degree that you want, or as fast. That doesn't mean that you give up on them.

Daily Habits

Of course I have daily habits to keep me in the frame of mind I desire. I get up early every morning and always have breakfast. I have oatmeal almost every day to keep my mind fresh. I write things down on index cards, which I keep with me. Daily habits like these provide structure to keep you in the right frame of mind during your day.

I do a little reading in the morning to make me feel good. *Guideposts* magazine has a verse for the day, and it's amazing to read it and feel that it was written for you. I also read some works of a spiritual nature before I go to bed.

When I get off work, the first thing I do is change my clothes and walk for at least four miles. I probably don't miss one day a month; I always find a way to get it in. In the wintertime, I have a pass to a recreation center at the gymnasium, which has a walking track above. I can look down and watch girls and boys practice basketball or some other sport. When I leave the office, the first thing I have on my mind is going to the recreation center. You make time for it, and it becomes a habit.

My daughter does the same thing. She walks every day, sometimes in the morning, sometimes in the evening, but she gets it in. It's our routine, and although it becomes a habit, I think it's a healthy one. Some people think of their routines as dull, saying, "I've got to go to work Monday." I think, "I *get* to go." That's a big difference.

I recently got a message from a woman who had been the CFO at my bank for years. She asked, "How can you stand all this foul language on TV?" I said, "I will give you the quickest answer in the world. Don't turn your TV on, and pick up a book."

I came home one day and told my wife that I had met with an attorney. She wanted to know if there was trouble. I said, "No. I'm going to start a cable company."

"That's hard to believe," she said. "You don't even watch TV."

"But it looks like everybody else is."

You look up the statistics: an average person watches six to eight hours of television a day. One of Hill's quotes is, "Tell me what you're doing with your spare time, and I'll tell you what you're going to amount to in life." You can become a brain surgeon if you put in enough years of studying and work.

There was a woman who worked for me. She was a physical wreck, and I hired her out of sympathy because she was a good friend of some of my employees, and I needed someone. She had trouble keeping it together.

She had lost a son when he was nine years old. He went to the hospital, went into a coma and died. She told me, "Nobody can tell you, 'I know the way you feel,' if you've ever lost a child. Nobody knows how you feel. They mean well, but they don't."

She was a pretty girl who sang in a church choir. She sat at a desk and did secretarial work for me. Every time I looked at her, mascara was streaming down her face. I would ask, "What's wrong with her today?" It was her son's birthday, or it was his first day in school, and those things came back to her, even though he'd been dead for a couple of years.

One day I asked her, "What would you like to be doing?"

"I'd give anything if I could finish college and teach little ones. I love to be around kids."

"Why don't you?"

"I can't quit work, because we're paying for a house, and we need two incomes."

"You can go back to take night classes."

"It will probably take me three, four, or five years. I don't know how much of a load I could take, but I'd be much older."

"Let me ask you a question," I said. "How old will you be if you *don't* go to school?"

"I would be the same age," she said, and when she realized what she said, she started laughing

I said, "You go on and go to school. I'm going to pay for it. You've got no excuses. If you don't go back, don't mention it anymore, because you've gotten an opportunity."

That was around twenty-five or thirty years ago, because she's about to retire. She taught the little ones. On occasions, she had me out to talk to them, and they were crawling all over the place. I said, "Gosh, you've got to have a knack for that."

She had a daughter too, who was younger than her son. She grew up, went to college, and became a schoolteacher, so both mother and daughter teach school.

It is possible to face the challenge and go on. As Mr. Stone told us, "You can't reason away worry." You can substitute something for it so that it becomes a passion, something that will occupy your time and your mind to get away from what's bothering you. Fear is the biggest deterrent to success—fear of the unknown, even if it's just a simple fear of traveling. It's not meant to be a stumbling block, it was meant to be a stepping-stone, but many people simply don't want to face it, because they look for a negative outcome rather than a positive one.

If you read or watch the news, you hear about the levels of anxiety in the culture, which seem to be at epidemic levels. We're an amped-up society now, and this has become a real problem. Yet studies say that only 5 percent of our daily worries are real; 95 percent never come to pass. It would be helpful if people could separate the 5 percent from the 95 percent, because a lot of them are probably thinking that they're worrying about something important. What is a good strategy for focusing only on your legitimate worries? How do you discard that other 95 percent?

Someone once said that in the later part of his life, he discovered that nearly all the things that he worried about never came to pass, and he could do nothing about the ones that did.

I think it's a matter of breaking it down. First, I would ask, what's the worst that could happen? Is it really important? And then, is there something I can do about it? Because you can't reason it through.

When someone is unfriendly to you, you can sit and worry about it, but you don't know what the person is going through. In any case, you can't let it bother you. Remember, there's basically nothing we can do to control what other people say to us, but we can control how we react. If we learn to do that, we'll find that we've got very few problems in life. If there's nothing we can do to solve a problem, we've got to get it out of our minds by concentrating on something else.

We learn it a thousand times in our reading: simply keep your mind on the things you want and away from things that you do not want. We do have a choice. We can sit down and do some planning; we can work on goals for which we have a passion. We can't be working on something with a passion and worrying at the same time. We get to choose. Do I spend my time concentrating on what I want to happen, or do I sit and think about something bad that I most likely can't do anything about?

Take the world situation. There's a poem written by a man a hundred years ago. He said he wanted to change the world. He found out he couldn't. He wanted to change his state, but he couldn't. He wanted to change his family, but he couldn't. He discovered that if he changed himself, starting with his inner thoughts, he could change his family. By changing his family, he could change his community, and by changing the community, he could change the world. It all starts with us individually. The outside simply reflects what we are on the inside, good or bad.

FOUR

Purpose and Belief

Let's delve a little deeper into beliefs. Often we can outline the best purpose and we can outline goals for ourselves, but we're held back by our beliefs—either about ourselves or about the world. Belief often seems deeply ingrained, almost like something in the nervous system that may have been conditioned over and over in childhood; at times it can be very difficult to dislodge. Let's talk about how we form those beliefs, what we say to ourselves, and the thoughts we allow to occupy our mind.

Rhonda Byrne's 2006 book *The Secret* discussed the law of attraction, which says that our self-talk and thoughts attract good or bad results into our lives, like a self-fulfilling prophecy.

Actually this wasn't a new discovery at all. Napoleon Hill discussed the law of attraction in many of his works. He first wrote about it in the March 1919 issue of *Hill's Golden Rule Magazine*. It goes back a long, long time. In simple terms, it's like attracts like—good or bad.

But I think you have to go back a little bit farther than that. You have to go back to your passion, your purpose. The Bible tells us that we must find our purpose. There's a wonderful quote from Oprah Winfrey saying it's our job to find our purpose, then go forward. People who don't have one are like drifting tumbleweed. Hill compared the mind to a fertile garden. It doesn't matter how good the soil is, if it's not tended, weeds will come up. This simply means that we watch our thoughts and actions until they become habits, but it has to start with finding a purpose in life.

Do you want to be a doctor? Do you want to be a veterinarian? Do you want to be a schoolteacher? If a passion drives you powerfully enough, you overlook all the roadblocks in front of you. You realize that it will be hard work and a long road, but you simply take one step at a time. It's just like a GPS: without those directions, we drift. Again, it's extremely important—you can't say it enough—to keep our minds on what we want and off what we don't want.

Hill taught us about the ability to choose, which makes all the difference. Hopefully, most of time we're choosing right. Hill talks about our dominant thoughts, which will determine where we end up in life, whether in success or mediocrity or failure.

It's important to distinguish a belief from a wish. As I see it, a belief has to do with something that you not only hope for but expect to accomplish. You expect results, whereas with wishes, you can say you'd like for it to happen, but basically you're not going to do anything about it: "I wish I had a lot of money." A wish doesn't get you anywhere. It has to be more than a wish.

A belief starts off with faith and confidence in yourself. Although you might start with some slight doubts, as you work towards your goal and you accomplish part of it, each step gives you confidence. You've got to be doing something that takes you closer to what you want. You might say you're on the right road, but if you're not moving, you'll get run over.

In 1930, Hill wrote an article for the *New York Post*. It's a huge article; it takes up almost a whole page. I laminated it and put it on the door of my archives. In it he talks about gaining self-confidence. It starts off with having a purpose, something that you have a passion about. Then it's a matter of having a belief that you can accomplish it, having faith that you can do it. To solve a problem or obtain what you want, belief is necessary: if you believe it won't happen, you simply won't put the effort out. Why would you?

You can just sit there on the sofa and think about ideas, but ideas in themselves are absolutely useless. You can have the best ideas in the world—whether they're about creating a new product or writing a book or anything else—but if you don't believe you can accomplish them, you're not going to do anything. You'll think, "Yes, I'd like to have that, but why waste my time? It'll never happen." With that attitude, it *will* never happen.

You've got to say, "This is what I'm going to do." This is the reason I discussed writing down goals. It's a contract with yourself. It's not someone saying, "Son, I want you to be a doctor or a minister." That's someone else giving you outside information. It's *you* making the decision: "I want to become a doctor. I want to become a lawyer." If we work toward a goal with passion, it's only natural to believe that we'll be able to accomplish it.

Negative Past, Positive Future

Someone reading this might say, "Don, you seem like a really positive person. You've had a wonderful life. You said you had a great childhood. Well, let me tell you about my childhood, Don. I was raised by a single parent who was an alcoholic. I didn't know my other parent." Maybe a mother or father died young, left the family, or went through bankruptcies. Some kids might have grown up in a difficult upbringing, in a very bad neighborhood, with drugs all around them. They may think, "It's easy for him to say, 'Just put your focus here,' but nothing in my life supports the possibility of a positive outcome."

The first thing I would say to them is, the greater the adversity, the greater the reward and the sweeter the results, because you've had to put effort out and you can look back. Furthermore, you're among the luckiest people on earth just to be born in the United States, because the opportunities are absolutely unbelievable. We have to learn to see them. If the ship doesn't come in, swim out to where it is. If nobody offers you a job, ask for one. Ask for favors and learn to not take no for an answer, but you can't continue just making excuses.

I remember a TV program in which a little girl of around twelve years old was always fussing, "Mommy didn't do this and didn't do that." Her mother finally told her: "I didn't have the instructions. I did the best I could with what I had."

I wasn't born in a rich family. Is that my parents' fault? They worked hard, and they considered themselves successful. They had lower standards than we have today. They thought a high-school education was absolutely great. When Napoleon Hill was growing up in the late nineteenth century, schooling wasn't mandatory in the State of Virginia. There were only about twenty high schools in the state, and they were just for boys. Boys would get a job in a coal field or a lumber business, and the girls got married. Some of us came along and said, "Is this all there is?"

My dad worked in a coal mine and made a good living, but the life expectancy for a coal miner at that time was about twenty years less than for other men. It's dangerous. I thought, "Gosh, I'm not lazy, but these guys are doing this work, and they're just making a living. Other people are using their brains and getting rich."

It really comes down to how badly you want something. Excuses don't get you anywhere. Sure, your parents were alcoholics, but it doesn't mean you have to be one. Yes, you do have a greater challenge, but as I said, the further you climb out on a limb to get the apple, the sweeter the fruit is. Whereas a lot of kids from wealthy families are complete wrecks. They cannot handle being born with a so-called success that they didn't earn.

I think it's good to see that we can take one step at a time. Of course, we can't all do it by ourselves, but we feel, "Yes, I've accomplished something."

My Dad's Self-Reliance

My dad contracted a disease later in life that partially disabled him. He had a seventh-grade education, but he was mechanically inclined, so he put levers on his car down to the brakes, and he could drive.

It might have been easy for my dad to sit around and watch television all day without doing anything, but he took lessons in basket weaving. He sat and made baskets and earned thousands of dollars. He didn't need the money—he had good retirement benefits and savings—but it put him in communication with other people. They would come to his home, talk to him, and buy some baskets. I kept telling him, "Dad, you're selling them too cheaply; people are reselling them." He said, "Oh, that's OK." He got a big article written about him, and he got a letter from the governor of the state, congratulating him for his ability.

When I was a bank president, I had a big credenza, and I had Dad's baskets sitting up on top of it, because I was proud of them. They were beautiful baskets, which I used for various things. One day an attorney came to my office and saw them. He said, "You know the woman that works for me? She's got one of those baskets. She said her daddy made it."

"Greg," I said, "we've got the same father."

"Gosh, I didn't know that," he said. "I see you pick her up for lunch occasionally, but I didn't think anything about it."

"Well, that's my sister, and my only sister, and she's an absolute angel."

I visited my dad one Saturday and noticed that the car was gone, but the door was open. I went in. He was lying on the kitchen floor. I said. "Dad, what's wrong?" He said that some unit in the refrigerator was burned out. He lay on the floor and took it out. He told Mom what he needed and where to buy it. He just lay there on the floor until she got back so he could fix it.

He was as independent as all get-out. He changed his own oil and greased his vehicle. He mowed his own grass, he raised flowers, and he just stayed busy. Some of the neighbors didn't drive, or were old. He would take them to the doctor or the hospital, or he would take them grocery shopping. Even though he was partly paralyzed, he had the use of his hands, and he had the use of his mind.

It has a lot to do with the way we interpret things. Say this book comes out, and we submit a query to five hundred foreign publishers. We get responses from twenty or thirty who want to see it and end up doing five or ten contracts. Do I think about the contracts I end up with, or do I think about the other hundreds that never replied? That's left up to me.

In my opinion, happiness is not a goal. It even sounds a bit stupid: "I want to be happy." OK—jump up and down all you want. Happiness comes from the satisfaction of doing something, whether it's playing with your grandkids, reading a good book, or taking a trip. Maybe it does start with our thought processes. It's like going on a trip: the anticipation—knowing what we're going to do—is sometimes more satisfying than the trip itself. Even so, satisfaction is the result not so much of thinking as of doing. Go ahead and think happiness, but the happiness will come to you because of what you're doing.

Beliefs about Money

In my estimation, money is a poor ultimate goal, because people who concentrate on money may do things that are not right. I think money should come to us by doing something we enjoy.

There are only two legitimate ways to make money: selling either a product or a service. If we provide an excellent service or an excellent product, the money will be the result of what we're doing rather than a goal in itself. Again, you can look at money in two different ways: do you have it, or does it have you? When money determines your every act, I don't think you'll develop a feeling of gratitude. I don't think you will ever have happiness until you discover that the money's only a tool. Yes, you can have a better life, but you can also make a difference in the lives of other people or of causes of your own choosing. You can have $1 million and be happy, or you can have $20 million and be unhappy. I think if you're rewarded for the results of what you've accomplished, then the money is a byproduct. It'll be very satisfying to you. You will find places where the money can be used to make it better for other people's lives.

FIVE

Desire and Discipline

Discipline, I think, starts with what you're driven by. One time I remember an executive saying he was having trouble with his weight, so he took up running. He said he hated it, but he disciplined himself. One time he was running in the rain, and all of a sudden it hit him how happy he was to be out there.

When you first start doing something and visualize the results that you're going to get, it makes the process easier. Various people say that it takes a certain number of days—some say fourteen; some say fifty-six—for something to become a habit. I don't know how they arrive at these figures, but I do know if you repeat an activity such as exercise, it will come more easily each time. It becomes a routine, and we will do it almost automatically.

If your desire is strong, you will have the discipline to stick with it. People are in prison for one reason: lack of discipline. If you don't have discipline, you'll end up in a place where they feed you *what* they want to feed you *when* they want to feed you. These people lacked just one thing in life: they never disciplined themselves, and they've ended up at a place where discipline is imposed upon them. They never thought far enough ahead about what would happen to them.

Of course, a lot of people want the rewards of discipline immediately, even though sometime they're way down the road. I don't even know how much exercise will improve your life, but I know that it's going to do so. Some things happen that are beyond our control, but there are lots of things we can do to improve our odds.

It's just like being obese: you can be thirty years old and be so large that you can't sit at an airplane seat. Practically always there's only been one thing lacking: you never disciplined yourself with your food or your exercise.

The problems both of money and weight are really solved by third-grade math. If you're too heavy, there are two ways you can deal with your problem. One is eat less, and the other is burn more calories. Either one will make improvements, but if you do them both, you'll get there faster.

Money is the same. It's third-grade math: if you spend more money than you make, you're going to get in trouble. There are two ways of solving the problem: you can spend less, and you can make more money. If you can do them both at the same time, you'll get there more quickly, but in any case discipline is simply a matter of third-grade math. That's all it is.

Some people never develop discipline, and they lead miserable lives. Say someone tells you, "Let's go to that new restaurant," and you say, "I hear it's quite expensive." They'll say, "Yes, it is, but the food is wonderful." Then you say you'll go in a couple of weeks, when you get your check from the government. That's not leading a good life.

Sometimes people overcomplicate discipline. Every year dozens of diet books come out with all sorts of different formulas: the carbohydrate diet, the protein diet, and so on. My wife said that once the ladies in the beauty shop were discussing a new diet. A woman went on and on about how easy it was and how much weight people lost on it. Finally someone asked her, "Where did you read that?" It was in a pulp magazine, which may not have been the best source.

In her later life, Liz Taylor put on lots of weight. They put her picture on the cover of a pulp magazine, and that was the best-selling issue they'd ever had, because women who were having trouble with their weight could look at it and say, "Liz Taylor was one of the prettiest women in the world. Now look at her. I don't feel so bad about myself." I guess misery loves company, although I don't know what good that does you.

Sometimes I've had conversations with people who were behind financially. Several of them would tell me, "I bet I'm not the only one behind." I've said, "You take care of your own problem. If everybody in town loses their house and you lose yours too, are you going to feel better?"

A lot of people feel better when they think, "I'm not the only one who has been bankrupt," or "I'm not the only one who's been broke." I don't know why you should feel any better because other people are in a miserable condition too. You're responsible for yourself; you're not responsible for the other people.

The Discipline of Napoleon Hill

I think Napoleon Hill was disciplined, at least in some areas. He was particular about his food and his health, and he lived to be eighty-seven. He followed a pretty strict routine for most of his life. He smoked a cigar occasionally, and he said sometimes he had a drink or two, but they never caused him problems.

Hill may have been lacking in financial discipline, at least in the beginning—the Rolls-Royce, the six-hundred-acre estate in the Catskills. He probably thought it was necessary for him to show that his methods worked. He had lots of problems. He went through the Depression and World War II. It wasn't easy. He made money, but he never learned to manage it. He thought it was more a show of success: he never took the long approach to it.

But as I said, he met Annie Lou in 1941 and married her in 1943, and he had twenty-seven good years afterward. Annie Lou, who had done bookkeeping, had the finances down pretty well.

Basically, it was in his last years that Hill accomplished most of his best work and left a legacy. He wanted to set up a nonprofit to continue his principles and teach them all over the world. He could have sold his copyrights to his books and accumulated a lot of cash, but he chose not to. He chose to create a nonprofit and give it the rights to his books so that it could carry on his mission.

SIX

Mentoring and Learning from Others

Mentoring was a big part of Napoleon Hill's teaching. In Master Mind groups, he said, people would be mentored by others and gain experience from them, rather than just relying on their own experience.

As I've said, there are two ways we learn, and one is association with other people. Recently I talked to the guy who gave me my job in banking back in 1975, and we were discussing new technology. He told me about a new substance called graphene, which may take off over the next ten years. It's already being used in golf balls, but it will be used in other items, such as cell phones. For vehicles, it's lighter, stronger, and more durable than fiberglass or steel. The problem is that it's expensive, and they haven't produced it yet at an affordable cost.

In any case, you can learn from other people. Monkeys learn from monkeys, so people can learn from people. It's a pleasure to sit around and listen to people, because we don't learn anything when we're doing the talking.

Teaching a class causes me to learn too, because I study up on the subject. With Napoleon Hill's seventeen principles of success, I try to give students not only the information but some examples that they can relate to.

Especially with younger people, I think the main part is simply to inspire them. When I wrote a book, I hoped there was at least one young person who could read it and say, "If that dumb old boy can make it, maybe there's a chance for me also."

Recently on the campus of the University of Virginia at Wise, where our offices are, I met a young man. I spoke to him and said, "I've not seen you before. What class are you in?"

"I'm a freshman," he said.

We talked for a couple minutes. I told him where my office is and said, "If you ever need a good book to read, stop by."

"Can I come by some morning?"

"Yes."

He was there the next morning. I got to talk to him a few minutes and gave him a book, and he left feeling really good. I've seen him two or three times since then, because the dorms are close by. I'm hoping he does something with the book.

College is a big change. My mentor Dr. Smiddy said, "I feel bad about young people who come to the college, but they've left their minds back home." In other words, they weren't mentally prepared to make the change.

My daughter went to Virginia Tech for four years. She's an only child; she was always with us; we didn't go anywhere we couldn't take our daughter. When she was at college, we talked to her every day. This was twenty-nine years ago; my phone bill was $400 or $500 a month. She'd come home every weekend, or we went to see her, for the whole four years. When she went away to college, she knew it would be tough for her to break away, but that was the first step.

When my daughter got out, she was a CPA, and she ended up traveling for Brinks, doing audits for them all over the country. That was a good experience for her, to be able to travel a lot. Susan Jeffers summed it up in the title of her book: *Feel the Fear and Do It Anyway*. Action will remove our fears; thinking won't.

My good friend Jim Stovall wrote a book called *The Millionaire Map*. If you just remember one sentence from it, it would be this: be sure that you use a map by someone who's been where you want to go.

I see a lot of people out there mentoring without being qualified. For example, if your brother-in-law has just come out of bankruptcy court, you probably don't want to pay a lot of attention to what he says about finances. I have personal acquaintances who have been financial risks, but they're handing out a lot of advice.

I use a quote from Henry David Thoreau: "I never sit down to write until I've stood up and lived." Don't be talking about something unless you've demonstrated that it works. I think that's absolutely the first criterion. I've listened to people like Bill Gates and Warren Buffett because they've done things that work. I think I can learn about stocks from Warren Buffett. I can see what he's bought and his reasoning behind it. His advice is coming from an unselfish place. He's not trying to make money from me.

The same advice doesn't always work for the same people. For example, you can take a lot more financial risk when you're younger. Yes, you listen to people, and you read and study the periodicals. There are some common-sense things that you'll hear from most people—about diversification and not having too much money in cash—but it's really important to get to the point where you can make your own decisions.

In the end, the most important money you'll ever invest is in yourself. The second most important investment is in your family and your employees. That's where you'll get the best results.

You have to remember that the person who is selling real estate wants to sell real estate. It may or may not be the best thing for you. The person selling gold wants to sell you gold because he makes money from it. You've got to consider their motives.

I think the best thing you can do is educate yourself, learn from these people, and make your own decision. I've never told anybody what stock to buy. Someone might say, "Don Green told me to buy a stock, and I lost all this money," but he's not very likely to say, "He told me about this stock, and I've made all this money." People will shift the blame to someone else: "My broker told me to buy this." Well, the broker suggested it, but do you make your own decisions? Even if you make mistakes, you look at them as learning experiences.

When I was a bank president, we had a cafeteria upstairs, although I never used it. I never fraternized with the employees, because if you have sixty employees and you continue to take one lady out to lunch, the rest of them will wonder what's going on and let their imaginations run wild.

One of the loan officers told me that some of the female employees were sitting at a table and discussing money. One of them asked, "How much money do you try to keep as a minimum in your checking account?" Another woman replied, "We don't ever discuss money."

Now these are people that no doubt discuss their love lives and everything else, yet they could not discuss money. Sometimes I counsel people who are having trouble with finances; they tell me that they're living with someone and they can't discuss money. That's kind of amazing.

The Master Mind Principle

In regard to the Master Mind group, let's start by talking about what it is *not*. It is not a group of people getting together, drinking beer, and discussing what they are going to accomplish in life.

Napoleon Hill mentions the case of Andrew Carnegie. He came over to this country as a young boy with only part of a grade-school education. Yet he formed U.S. Steel: it was the largest steel company, because he consolidated all of the others into it. People thought he bought them up to control the prices, but he actually cut prices tremendously. He basically led the Age of Steel, because he made steel in such a way that it could be used in many places. Carnegie used the Master Mind by assembling the chemists, the lawyers, the accountants, and all the other people necessary to put his enterprise together.

The Master Mind is defined as two or more minds acting in perfect harmony for a common goal. You can have meetings, advisors, or what have you. Each one in the group may have their own idea—one wants to open a grocery store, another wants to build something. They can learn from one another, but according to Napoleon Hill, this is not a Master Mind. One essential characteristic of a Master Mind group is harmony, and the other is that they have a common problem they're trying to solve. That makes all the difference in the world.

Andrew Carnegie built U.S. Steel, because he knew how to put people together. In one case, he hired a chemist from abroad. Carnegie thought this chemist was the brightest guy he could get, but he did not work in harmony with the others. What did Carnegie do—let everybody else go? No, he replaced the person who was disruptive, who was not in harmony. It's a tremendous example of accomplishment to make steel and make it affordably. By using the Master Mind principle, all working towards a common goal, they had excellent results.

I think the Master Mind could be applied in different manners, but it's not a get-together bull session, where everybody throws ideas out for fifteen different items. There's nothing wrong with doing this; probably you'll learn from it. But it's not a true Master Mind by Napoleon Hill's definition.

SEVEN

Favorite Ideas and Stories

Think and Grow Rich was published in 1937, at the height of the Depression. Hill said that it was written for the millions of men and women who were living in poverty and in fear of poverty.

Persistence

In some ways, this book is really a story about persistence. In chapter 1, Hill tells the story of Edwin Barnes. He was a tramp, but he had a desire: to partner with the great inventor Thomas Edison. Hill told the story of Barnes and the way he went about realizing his desire. Hill said that if he could convey that message to the reader, the reader would not need to read the rest of the book.

I've got a number of letters from later in Hill's life, handwritten letters from Barnes. They kept in communication all that time, and they had nicknames for each other. Barnes called him "Nap the Sap" and other different names.

Barnes had a desire and, above all, persistence. He looked like a tramp and he had to hitchhike, but he became Edison's only partner because he had a desire to be his partner and he never let up. He headed up the Dictaphone project; Edison gave it to him to sell to businesses.

I also love the story of the nine-year-old girl at the old mill. She goes to the mill and says, "My mammy has got to have 50 cents." The man keeps telling her, "No." She never takes her eyes off him, and she keeps saying, "My mammy's got to have 50 cents." Finally he tells her, "I'm going beat you with a stick," but she keeps saying, "My mammy has got to have 50 cents." Finally he gives her 50 cents. She backs away up to the door, afraid that he is really going to hit her.

The man said after that happened, he stared out the window for a minute, realizing that he just been conquered by a nine-year-old kid. The little girl might not have known what persistence was, but she practiced it. She took the threat of a beating with a stick to get that 50 cents. That's a common theme throughout the book.

Of course, there's the story of Hill's son Blair, who was born without ears. Hill never let him go to a school for the deaf and dumb. The doctors told him to just get over it; he was never going to be able to hear, but Hill practiced autosuggestion with him. Finally he recovered 65 percent of his normal hearing and led a normal life. He went to college, became a businessman, and served on a bank board in West Virginia. That's a story of persistence if there ever was one.

That's a common theme in the book. Hill demonstrates over and over again that people become successes just through persistence. As Steve Jobs says, "About half of what separates the successful entrepreneurs from the nonsuccessful ones is pure perseverance." His biography tells about his persistence in developing and cofounding Apple. A lot of other people today developed their persistence out of *Think and Grow Rich*.

Concentration and Autosuggestion

Desire, persistence, accurate thinking, and the Master Mind are principles that stand out in *Think and Grow Rich*. Another important one is concentration. This simply means keeping your mind on what you want and off what you don't want.

Napoleon Hill arrived at the thirteen steps to riches that he outlines in *Think and Grow Rich* after doing five hundred interviews. From these, he simply concluded that these were the things that these successful people did. Elsewhere he said that he often learned more from failures—that is, knowing what *not* to do, which is just as important as knowing what to do. He said he did over ten thousand interviews overall. Of course, a lot of these were simply questionnaires that the interviewees filled out and sent back to him.

Incidentally, the important principle of going the extra mile is not explicitly in either *Law of Success* or *Think and Grow Rich*. The idea is there, but the actual words "go the extra mile" first appeared in one of the other books, How to Sell Your Way through Life, published in 1939.

Another important principle, which I don't think is emphasized enough, is autosuggestion. In fact, the most important conversation we'll ever have in our life occurs through autosuggestion. That's how we develop our beliefs—by talking to ourselves, picturing what we want to accomplish, and repeating certain ideas to ourselves. These things become part of our subconscious.

What do you say when you talk to yourself? For example, someone can tell you that you'll never run a marathon, but you can shake that off and mentally tell yourself, "I'll show them." But when *you* say to yourself, "I'm not in shape to run a marathon," you will tend to believe it, even if it's a lie. It's absolutely essential to talk to ourselves in the right manner.

So much of it is in the mind. I've been into two putting contests my life, and I won one and tied the other. I can putt well, because I have the belief that when I get up there, the ball is going to go in the hole. Why would you get up there and say, "I never could putt?"

If I'm going to play with someone, I want to say something positive about myself. I read Harvey Penick's book on golf, and he says, "There are only two things that are involved in putting: one of them is location, and the other one is speed."

First off, in your mind, pick a spot that you're going to putt to. Then, when you're getting ready to hit it, decide how hard: you need to hit it ten feet or whatever. When people tend to get behind the ball, they bounce back and forth between these two decisions: "Where do I hit? How hard do I hit?" If part of your mind is bouncing back and forth, you look goofy. But if you concentrate, you should be relatively close, no matter how the putt turns out.

If the putt doesn't turn out right, many people will tell themselves, "I don't know why I have never learned how to putt." Why would you want to say that to yourself? That's fixing to fail.

The Great Moneymaking Secret

Here's a question I get sometimes. In the preface to *Think and Grow Rich*, Hill states, "In every chapter of this book, mention has been made of the money-making secret which has made fortunes for more than five hundred exceedingly wealthy men whom I have carefully analyzed over a long period of years."

I've been asked what this secret is. Each of us can develop our own answers, but I can offer a couple of suggestions. In the first place, the central theme of all of his writings is that whatever the mind can conceive or believe, it can achieve. In the second place, there's the principle of action. Hill stresses having a burning desire, making a plan, and persisting. That means taking action. The word *action* appears seventy-seven times in *Think and Grow Rich*. That's what might jump out at you if you really study the book. I think the two of these pretty well account for Hill's secret, but he wanted readers to discover it on their own.

Of course, we can think of things that are not realistic: probably man will never be able to run a mile in two seconds. Even so, I think we can make use of the statement, "What the mind of man can conceive and believe, the mind can achieve." You can apply this concept to Marconi's wireless telegraph or the incandescent light bulb or any other great invention. Everything starts with an idea, but ideas themselves are worthless until you take the steps necessary for making them come about.

Hill emphasized learning by doing. For example, you can take a kindergarten teacher. She's got a bunch of youngsters and she's showing them how to make things with Play-Doh. If she makes little animals or balls or other different objects, she'll keep the youngsters' attention for a while. But if she really wants to do a good job, she's going to go to each one of them and give them a handful of Play-Doh. They're going to be much more satisfied with what they're able to do than with what she's done. They'll have a feeling of accomplishment, and they'll forget what time of day it is. It makes all the difference in the world to be involved in something rather than just having someone telling you to do it. Kids don't get a lot of satisfaction out of seeing somebody else do something. Even if they don't do a good job, they develop that feeling of "Hey, I did that myself. Look here I made a banana out of this Play-Doh," and that's what they'll remember.

The Writing of *Think and Grow Rich*

Hill started writing *Think and Grow Rich* in 1933 or 1934, possibly earlier. He finished it during his marriage to Rosa Lee Beeland, and she contributed to it with work on the subjects of cosmic habitforce and the transmutation of sexual energy. For a long time after their divorce, she was an editor for *Popular Mechanics*.

As Hill was writing the book, he was trying to tell the stories of his interviewees and what they believed had driven their success. The last thing he wrote was the title. His publisher told him that if he didn't come up with a title, they were going to call it *Use Your Noodle and Get the Boodle*, which was silly. In the end, he produced a title that speaks loud and clear: *Think and Grow Rich*.

Of course, the book was about money, with its steps to riches, but if you really read it and think about it, you could apply the same steps to achieving anything; it doesn't necessarily have to be money. You may, for instance, want to use these principles to do a scientific experiment or invent some labor-saving device. The same principles apply to anything you're trying to do.

Hill said in some of his writings that later someone would come along and improve what he did. Maybe so, but in my case, I've been careful; I still have the folders on each one of his seventeen principles of success. Although we relate to stories, the stories should be relevant today. If you're going to talk about persistence, use Steve Jobs; people today all have smartphones, so that means something to them. Or we might use Billy Ray Cyrus or Steve Harvey—people that readers can relate to. Whenever you can relate a current story to one of the principles, it's much easier to get the material across.

The Master-Key to Riches

Let me move on to another classic of Hill's: *The Master-Key to Riches*. He wrote it in 1945. By this time, he had married Annie Lou, so now he had money and was leading a comfortable life. If you study the book, it's obvious that his thinking had changed as far as money was concerned. In this book he lists the twelve great riches of life, but economic security is only number twelve.

The first of the great riches of life is a positive mental attitude. Second is sound physical health. We all know how important this is. He talks about health consciousness, which is produced by a mind that thinks in terms of health and not of illness; it also includes temperance of habits in eating and properly balanced physical activities.

The third of the riches is harmony in human relations. He said that this begins with oneself, and it's true. As Shakespeare wrote, "To thine own self be true, and it must follow, as the night the day, thou canst not then be false to any man."

Number four is freedom from fear. Of course, the first of all of the negative emotions is fear. Hill said, "No man who fears anything is a free man. Fear is a sign of evil. Wherever it appears man will find a cause which must be eliminated before you can become rich in the fuller sense."

Hill discussed the seven basic fears: (1) fear of poverty; (2) fear of criticism; (3) fear of ill health; (4) fear of loss of love; (5) fear of loss of liberty; (6) fear of old age; and (7) fear of death.

Number five of the twelve great riches was the hope of achievement. It's in all of us; we hope for better lives for ourselves and our children. He said it simply: "The greatest of all forms of happiness comes in our sense of the hope of achievement of some yet unattained desire."

The sixth is the capacity for faith. Hill said, "Faith is a connecting link between the conscious mind of man and a great universal reservoir of Infinite Intelligence. It is the fertile soil of the garden of the human mind wherein may be produced all the riches of life. It is the 'eternal elixir' which gives creative power and action to the impulse of thought. Faith is the basis of all so-called miracles."

The seventh of the twelve great riches is the willingness to share one's blessings. Hill wrote: "He who has not learned the blessed of art of sharing has not learned the true path to happiness. Riches which are not shared, whether they are material riches or the intangibles, wither and die like the rose on a severed stem, for it is one of Nature's first laws that inaction and disuse leads to decay and death, and this law applies to the material possessions of man just as it applies to the living cells of every physical body." He stresses both the obligation and the happiness of sharing our blessings with others.

Number eight is a labor of love. "There can be no richer man than he who has found a labor of love and who is busily engaged in performing it, for labor is the highest form of human expression of desire. Labor is the liaison between the demand and the supply of all human needs, the forerunner of all human partners, the medium by which the imagination of man is given the wings of action. And all labor of love is sanctified because it brings the joy of self-expression to whoever performs it."

Hill listed number nine as an open mind on all subjects. As I mentioned, he wrote a piece on tolerance. He said, "Tolerance, which is among the highest attributes of culture, is expressed only by the person who has an open mind on all subjects. And it is only the man with an open mind who becomes truly educated and who is prepared to avail himself of greater riches in life."

Number ten is self-discipline: "The man who is not the master of himself may never become the master of anything. He who is the master of self can become the master of his own earthly destiny, the 'master of his fate, the Captain of his soul.' And the highest form of self-discipline consists in the expression of humility of the heart when one has attained great riches or has been overtaken by that which is commonly called success." I think that's a tremendous discussion of self-discipline and what it does for us.

The eleventh one is the capacity to understand people. Hill wrote, "The man who is rich in the understanding of people always recognizes that all people are fundamentally alike in that they have evolved from the same stem; that all human activities are inspired by one or more of the nine basic motives of life," which he lists as (1) love; (2) sex; (3) the desire for material gain; (4) the desire for self-preservation; (5) the desire for freedom of body and mind; (6) the desire for self-expression; (7) the desire for perpetuation of life after death; (8) anger; (9) and fear.

Furthermore, he adds, "the man who would understand others must first understand himself. The capacity to understand others eliminates many of the common causes of friction among men. It is the foundation of all friendship. It is the basis of all harmony and cooperation among men. It is the fundamental of major importance in all leadership which calls for friendly cooperation. And some believe that it is an approach of major importance to the understanding of the Creator of all things."

Number twelve, I think, is really interesting: economic security. *Think and Grow Rich* was about money, "for men and women who resent poverty." By the time he wrote *The Master-Key to Riches*, only eight years later, he had gone through a divorce that left him broke, followed by a happy marriage that lasted for twenty-seven years. By this point, he'd learned that economic security is not the most important thing. Nor is it the least important; it is simply the "tangible portion" of the twelve riches.

"Economic security is not attained by the possession of money alone," wrote Hill. "It is attained by the useful service one renders, for useful service may be converted into all forms of human needs, with or without the use the money.

"Henry Ford has economic security, not because he controls a vast fortune of money, but for the better reason that he provides profitable employment for millions of men and women and also dependable transportation by automobile for still greater numbers of people. The service he rendered has attracted the money he controls, and it is in this manner that all enduring economic security must be attained."

In the end, human relations and service to humanity are primary. That is the mission statement for the Napoleon Hill Foundation: making the world a better place in which to live. Focusing on human relations is the best step we can take, because we all have basic wants, such as hope of attainment and a desire for friendship, cooperation, being with other people, and being liked.

Hill tries to point out the things that help get us there. For example, if we understand human relations, we won't be so quick to judge someone else or make decisions about other people. As they say, don't judge a man until you've walked a mile in his moccasins. We can be too quick to judge someone when we don't know their story or what their problem is. They may just need some encouragement. They may just need a friend.

There is the saying: "Make a friend: be a friend." As Hill developed, he grew more interested in a satisfying life. As he went along—and we see this all the way up to his death—he became ever more interested in this aspect of life: his last book was *Grow Rich with Peace of Mind*. Obviously he evolved from thinking about basically nothing but money to being involved with other people and helping them have a good life.

So if you wanted to get a fuller picture of Napoleon Hill, you should read *Think and Grow Rich* together with *The Master-Key to Riches*.

Success through a Positive Mental Attitude

The next book I want to discuss is a favorite of mine. Hill coauthored it with W. Clement Stone, who was, as we've seen, the original backer of the Napoleon Hill Foundation. The book is called *Success through a Positive Mental Attitude*.

Stone had never met Hill, although he had read his books. Stone went to Chicago for a dental convention, and Hill was there, although Stone said he didn't realize Hill was still alive. At this point Stone's insurance company had grown astronomically, because Hill's book was required reading for all of his employees. Stone gave away thousands of copies of the book. As his company grew, he would bring in speakers, including Hill and many of the other big names of the day, to address his seven thousand employees.

Hill and Stone used to have discussions about the importance of a positive mental attitude, and eventually they did this book together. Of course, Stone had written some on his own, and he later wrote two books, *Believe and Achieve* and *The Success System That Never Fails*. Later still, he wrote a book called *The Other Side of the Mind*, which gets into psychic phenomena. It's an interesting book; the Napoleon Hill Foundation has the copyright to it.

Stone grew up as an only child; his mother was a seamstress. He sold newspapers on the street. When he was six years old, the bigger boys would beat him up because they claimed he was on their corner. Then he began selling papers in a restaurant. They threw him out, but he kept going back; finally the patrons said, "Leave him alone." All of a sudden, he had a restaurant he could go to every morning to sell papers. That was persistence. Another characteristic he developed was faith. His mother taught him to kneel at the bed and give thanks, no matter how late it was.

In the early 1950s, Hill was in semi-retirement. Stone challenged him: "Let's go out and speak to people and teach this material."

Hill said, "I will, if you will be my general manager."

Stone took it on. They intended to do it for five years, but their partnership lasted ten years, from 1952 to 1962.

In 1959, Hill and Stone published *Success through a Positive Mental Attitude*. The book shows you how to use a positive mental attitude to rid your mind of cobwebs and how to set your sights on a goal and attain it through persistence and positive action. In simple, straightforward language, they present five self-motivators that provide a springboard to success; six steps to cheerfulness; and three ways to rid yourself of guilt. They urge you to start now in your ways of success in business and in your social life by reading what others have done and how they have done it. Remember that you can do it too.

When I reprinted this book in a collector's edition, Denis Waitley, author of *Seeds of Greatness* and *Psychology of Success*, gave an endorsement saying that it changed his life from that of an also-ran to that of a front-runner. If you want to be a winner, read it once a year. I do, and I learn something new from it each time.

Although *Success through a Positive Mental Attitude* was published over sixty years ago, it still sells tremendously well—probably around twenty million copies in its thirty-seven editions. That tells you something. Most other books disappear. They have a shelf life of a year, two years at most, when the royalties are good. You can't imagine getting royalties for something that's been out there for over sixty years.

The preface, by Og Mandino, begins by saying:

The great Danish philosopher and religious thinker, Søren Kierkegaard, once wrote, "It is the sign of a good book, when the book reads you."

You hold in your hands such a book, one that has not only become a classic in the self-help field, but also has that rare ability to relate to your problems, sympathize with them, and then advise you on their solutions as a wise old friend would.

Much of the book's message has to do with developing the right attitude—saying why something can be done rather than why it can't be done, thinking yes instead of thinking no.

In his preface, Mandino goes on to say, "If you truly wish to change your life for the better, and are willing to pay a price in time and thinking and effort to reach your goals—and if you're not kidding yourself—then you hold in your hands a diamond plucked from a beach of pebbles, a road map to a better future, a valuable blueprint that will enable you to complete and restructure your future."

This book helps you remove doubts and shift your mind from negative thinking to positive thinking. I think all the progress in the world has been made by people who think positively, believing that something *can* be done.

With a positive attitude, you will do what's necessary to succeed: you'll search, you'll study, you'll try and retry, and you'll stick with your objective. Your mind will stay on track rather than getting distracted. A positive mental attitude doesn't mean ego: "I can do anything." It's just self-confidence.

As Mandino and Kierkegaard say, the book reads you. That means that as you go through it, you ask, "How does this relate to me?" This is the use for the book. It's not a novel that you read to see what happens at the end. This is practical information that you can read and relate to your own life, asking yourself this vital question: how will this improve what I'm trying to do?

If this book can help move you from a negative state to a positive state, then it's accomplished its goal. That's the reason for going back and rereading it at different periods of life: to reacquaint yourself with the principles lest you get off track. Again, it's not a matter of ego: "I am the greatest ever." It's just a quiet feeling.

I remember that Mr. Stone used to say, "You've got problems? That's great. People get paid for solving problems, and the bigger the problem they solve, the more money they earn. The big earners in this country are people who solve big problems." In every difficulty is a seed of an equivalent or greater benefit. When we see something that's wrong, we start immediately looking at what can be done about it, how we can improve it, and how we can solve it. That's what people get paid for doing.

PMA: Positive Mental Attitude

At the end of each chapter of *Success through a Positive Mental Attitude*, Stone and Hill give some very specific and very helpful thoughts to guide readers. They speak of positive mental attitude, which they abbreviate as PMA. They offer ten recommendations for attracting happiness with a positive mental attitude.

I think all ten can be summed up by saying that to be happy, make others happy. But here are the others.

1. Abraham Lincoln once said, "It has been my observation that people are just about as happy as they make up their minds to be."

2. There are very few differences between people, but there are little differences that make a big difference. The little difference is attitude. The big difference is whether it's positive or negative.

3. One of the surest ways to find happiness is devote your energy towards making someone else happy.

4. If you search for happiness, you'll find it elusive, but if you try to bring happiness to someone else, it will return to you many times over.

5. If you share happiness and all that is good and desirable, you will attract happiness and the good and the desirable.

6. If you share misery and unhappiness, you'll attract misery and unhappiness to yourself. This all goes back to "like attracts like": we get what we send out. You don't get a smile from someone by frowning at them. It starts with sowing the thought, because what we plant comes back to us, oftentimes in much greater abundance.

7. Happiness begins at home. Motivate the members of your family to be happy, just as a good salesman motivates his prospects to buy.

8. When two forceful personalities are opposed and it is desirable that they live together in harmony, at least one must use the power of PMA.

9. Be sensitive to the reaction of others.

10. Learn to live contently in Happy Valley. This means being contented with your position in life as it is. That does not mean that we can't seek improvements. If we're not already in Happy Valley, these ten steps will get us there.

How to Sell Your Way through Life

Let me go on to Hill's *How to Sell Your Way through Life*, which is one of his less-known books. It was published in 1939, when he was still married to Rosa Lee Beeland. *How to Sell Your Way Through Life* is an excellent book on salesmanship.

My good friend Jeffrey Gitomer, author of *Little Red Book on Selling* (and one of today's best-selling sales authors), has one of the best collections of Napoleon Hill's material, and he gives a world of credit to *How to Sell Your Way through Life*. He said that that book meant the most to him, because each of us is selling something every day, whether it's to our children, our coworkers, or our employer. We're selling our personality. A lot of people say, "I can't sell anything." Well, they need to stop and think about it, because if you want to get anywhere in life, you're going to have to learn to sell yourself to others.

The best salesmen do not sell the product; they sell themselves. If it's a good product, it will sell itself. That applies to life insurance or cars or any other product or service. At the same time, you'd better sell yourself to the other person so they'll have enough confidence to make the sale. That's why this is such a great book, especially for people who are making a living selling products. But even if we're getting a job, we're selling ourselves (or at least we'd better). Are you selling yourself in a positive or a negative manner? People form opinions of us from the way we behave. If you're not in the profession of selling your ideas, you're selling your kids on a way to live, on moral values.

The first step in teaching personal selling is autosuggestion. You sell yourself through the conversations you have with yourself. At the beginning of his career, Zig Ziglar sold cookware. He would have cooking parties, but people weren't buying the cookware, they were buying the social aspect: somebody comes in and makes a good meal, and then they'd sign you to buy a $399 set of cookware that you could probably purchase in a discount store for $39. Customers were buying the story. Ziglar said that the first step is autosuggestion: selling yourself on what you are handling; if you don't believe in a product that you're selling, don't sell it.

When he was out driving to make sales calls, Zig said that he noticed he was making excuses: "I'm not going to stop at that house. It doesn't look like a very good house." Or he'd come to one and say, "They are probably ready to go to bed." He was driving around rather than having an attitude that could help him sell.

Mr. Stone, I think, contributed a lot to the success of positive mental attitude. He told a story once. An insurance salesman came in and asked him, "I'd like to have some leads. Can you furnish me some leads?"

Mr. Stone said, "Yes, if you come back later today, I'll get you some leads."

Mr. Stone gave the salesman a list of people with their addresses. He came back later and said, "That was wonderful. I've sold nine of them. Could you give me another list?"

"I'll tell you what to do," said Mr. Stone. "Here's a phone book. You sit down and you take one out of each letter. That's what I did. I just went through the phone book."

The difference was that the salesman went in with the attitude that these people were ready to buy. Before, he'd had the attitude of "I don't know if I can sell or not."

When the entertainer Mel Tillis was trying to make it in the music business, he sold Bibles door to door. He had a speech impediment. Someone asked him how he did it. He said he would knock on a door; usually a woman answered. He would be stuttering: "M-m-m-ma'am, I-I-I-I'm selling Bibles. Can I come in and talk to you? Can I read from it to you?" Of course, he got invited in. Even though he had a speech impediment, he had the right attitude: "This lady wants to buy the Bibles I'm selling." It's practically all in your attitude.

A man says, "When I'm at work, I keep worrying about how things are going at home. When I get home, I'm worried about things at work." Zig said, "You've worn your mind out with traveling. You bounce from one thing to another. You think in one direction and then in the other rather than doing an autosuggestion and telling yourself, 'I don't know the answers, but they're going to come to me.'"

It's like liking yourself. If you like yourself, you tend to like others. It starts with your own self. You can't have one attitude and display another. It'll come through whether you want it to or not.

A related point has to do with having faith and then acting on it. Hill said, "Faith constructs; fear tears down." The order is never reversed.

Grow Rich with Peace of Mind

Grow Rich with Peace of Mind, published in 1967, was one of Hill's last books, and it was the last one published before he died in 1970. In a way it represents the full blossoming of his thought. He became much more spiritual.

Hill had really evolved from where he started. He was born in the Appalachians, growing up in poverty and seeing poverty. In those circumstances it would only be natural to think of money, because it's the best solution to poverty—people learning how to make their own money and become self-reliant. That's what he initially concentrated on when studying successful people. He certainly enjoyed material things—the estate, the Rolls-Royce— but as he matured, he changed. He acknowledged that money was wonderful and served good purposes, but happiness was more important. We get happiness by doing things that we enjoy, as a result of what we're doing, not as a goal in itself.

Originally this book was entitled *Success and Something Greater*, and that was the title originally announced, but the publisher thought that *Growing Rich with Peace of Mind* was the key takeaway: yes, I've been successful, I've made the money, but what can I do that brings me peace of mind? As Hill explains, it's making life better for other people and helping worthy causes.

Hill changed his viewpoint on money as the only thing that matters. Maybe that's true when you don't have any, but money alone does not bring happiness. We can use money as a tool or as a detriment. We can help other people; we can make a difference in the world rather than just spend, spend, spend, because material happiness doesn't last very long. You should get to the point in your life where you realize that buying a new car is merely a matter of transportation, but that you can buy a simple book and give it to somebody, and it could change their life. That's a better definition of happiness than a new car, or at least it should be. We can fool ourselves by thinking money will make us happy. It will not.

We can have money, or money can have us. When money is telling you what kind of life to lead, you're probably going to be miserable, because all you're going to be thinking about is making more or losing what you already have.

I think Hill did a great job of maturing. He could have done it a whole lot faster, but considering his background and the Depression, World War II, and so forth—the main thing is that he did get there. He left us something to read to help us understand what it's all about, to give us a better perspective on the contribution we can make. That's why he set up the Napoleon Hill Foundation as a nonprofit instead of buying an airplane or whatever else you could do with a lot of money.

Hill had a desire for his principles to be taught all over the world. That's the reason for the foundation's mission statement of making the world a better place in which to live. We keep that in mind constantly. If I can help spread the material to Israel or Sri Lanka or Cambodia or Thailand, certain numbers of people are going to be inspired by that.

We say that we don't just offer study material; we can change your life. If we study enough and we can teach others, we can change their lives. They in turn can teach others. We believe, "I learn it. I teach it to someone, who learns to teach it to someone, who can change the world." One of us can't do it all, and the more people we have out there adopting these beliefs and putting it to use, the better off we're all going to be, because we all want to survive. We all have the same desires, even though we may have different manners.

It's extremely valuable material. It's affected millions of lives and still continues to. His books are more popular today than when he was alive.

If you want to summarize the difference between *The Master-Key to Riches* and *Grow Rich with Peace of Mind*, I think he started *Master-Key* when his thinking was changing. By the time he published *Grow Rich with Peace of Mind*—there was over twenty years' difference between the publication dates—he had matured much more. He understood a lot more. He's explaining what makes a well balanced life. As I've said, happiness is not a goal. It's simply the result of something good that we've accomplished; it's actually the result of a completed goal.

Rather than thinking, "I'm going to be happy, I'm going to be happy," we can say, "These are things I want to do. I can make a difference in myself. I can make a difference in my family. I can make a difference in my community." It's not just caring about ourselves. We care for ourselves, but we expand it into making a positive difference in other people's lives.

Don't judge me by how much money I've got or how many stocks or how much real estate I own. Measure what I have accomplished in life through my children. If I leave a large estate of millions of dollars and my kids are on drugs, have married three times, and are in trouble with the law, somewhere along the line I've failed. I have to assume responsibility for that.

What we do should continue through our children, because they've gotten a better start and have more knowledge and more opportunity than we had. To me, how that continues is extremely important, because you cannot feel happy with a $10 million stock portfolio when you have a son in jail and a daughter that's walking the streets.

Your results lie in the people on whom you had an effect, either positive or negative. We hope it is positive. Sportscaster Charles Barkley, who had been a professional basketball player, once said, "Children shouldn't grow up with a sports star as their hero. Anybody can dunk a basketball"—of course, he's including himself. "What they need is parents that they look to as heroes."

Of course, our egos can intrude, and we can go overboard by doing too much for our kids, but we can try to create wholesome growth. My daughter can admire what her dad has accomplished and what I have tried to do with my life. When your kids admire you from that standpoint, you think, "Maybe I'm doing something right." I don't mean that I gave her everything she wanted; I wanted her to learn to do some of the things I did well and avoid some of the things I did if they weren't so good. As Confucius said, "Give a man a fish and he'll eat a day; teach him to fish, and you feed him for a life." I look at material goods the same way. It shouldn't be our responsibility to think we must leave so many millions of dollars to our kids or spoil them when they're growing up.

I remember a girl who had some money in her family. At high school, she was driving a BMW convertible, with a big diamond around her neck.

"Boy," I said, "I feel sorry for the guy she marries."

People would say, "What do you mean?"

"Anticipation is a good portion of life. If she marries some boy and he brings her some flowers, she's going to say, 'You idiot. I've got a BMW. Look at the jewelry that I had when I got married.' She's going to be hard to please."

I believe I was right. I think she married and divorced three times, because a good portion of life is anticipation.

When we go to bed, wake up, anticipate what we're going to do, and feel good about it, it's not work. When it becomes work, maybe we ought to find something else to do, because nobody should be forced to do something that makes them unhappy. We should be doing things that lead to happiness rather than trying to seek happiness directly.

I hope the things in this book will inspire someone. Even if it's only one person, then to me it's worth the time. Thinking that we might have made a difference in somebody else's life—to me that's happiness, and when people don't have it, I really have empathy for them.

I think people can find happiness if they find something to feel passionate about that also makes a difference in someone else's life—whether it's curing cancer or cleaning up the neighborhood. There's so much you can feel passionate about, and the result will be happiness, I will guarantee you. You've got to have a feeling of, "I have made a little bit of difference." I think that's what gives us happiness.

Napoleon Hill's Spiritual Beliefs

As for Hill's religious beliefs, I think they were universalistic. His father was one of the founders of the little church he attended; as a matter of fact, it's still standing. My in-laws belonged to that same church. Even today, they don't use musical instruments, but they are great orators; they're very dramatic. I think he got many of his oratorical skills from there.

Hill had a universal sense of tolerance. He wanted to see the day when people weren't known as Gentiles or Jews, for religion, for their skin color. He wanted to reach everybody.

On Sundays, he enjoyed driving around in the car with his wife and listening to the Mormon Tabernacle Choir. The fact is, he did some work with the Mormon church in the 1930s. At one point he mentioned that the president of the church said that from that day forward, no Mormon would be on public welfare. Even though Hill wasn't a Mormon, he admired that in them: they would take care of each other, they wouldn't rely on the government, they would become more self-reliant and would help one another if need be.

Gandhi was one of the men Hill admired most. Although they weren't of the traditional faith, his books obviously appeal to everybody. He made it clear that we all have different belief systems, even in regard to solving problems. This doesn't mean that one way is necessarily better than others.

If you and I go to lunch, we can take either the back roads or the interstate; there are many different routes to get you there.

Which one is the best? Well, one gets me there the fastest. Another one is the most scenic. Often when my wife and I traveled, we'd get off the interstate and travel on the back roads, because on the interstate, you see a lot of trucks, but you don't see a whole lot else. On the smaller roads, we'd see little antique places or some other attractions that were worth stopping for. The main thing is that we do have a choice.

EIGHT

Conclusion

Some of you may interested in knowing a little bit more about the Napoleon Hill Foundation. We're on the campus at University of Virginia at Wise—a beautiful campus. The college has been such a blessing to so many. I think 85 percent of the students today still require financial assistance, because most all of them, like me, are in the first generation of their family who went to college.

Education is a bridge to take these kids to where they want to go. Lack of education is the number one cause of poverty. Poverty is primarily caused by single women with children who are living without adequate support. They're not nurses, they're not schoolteachers; they don't have a profession that pays adequate money to properly take care of their children. That's why so many of them end up in trouble: they don't have a stable home life, because that's where it starts: we learn from our parents, good or bad.

At the same time, we can educate everyone. If a student becomes educated, it's pretty well-assured that their children will get those qualities too. Poverty breeds poverty. It's a matter of breaking that cycle. Most of the time you can assume that if a person went to college, their kids are more likely to go to college also.

On a personal basis, I try to inspire students. I love it when it's one on one, because I feel that if they sit and listen to me, maybe I can inspire them a little to get started. We've only got today: we can't undo yesterday, and tomorrow may never come. The sooner they start, the better off they are, and I try to teach them to say to themselves, "This what I'm going to accomplish." Once they start to develop belief and confidence that they can accomplish their goals, we can make suggestions to help them. You can't make them do it; you've got to talk to them and get them to see by giving examples. We give examples of people learning from defeat and overcoming adversity, whether it's a blind person or someone born without ears. No matter what the circumstances are, they can make a difference.

It starts inside; it starts with the way they think, because the whole process starts with action. As we've seen, it all starts with the thought process. In fact, we've got to do more than think;

we've got to plan. The plans might not be perfect, but we can learn from other people. If the plan doesn't work, you've failed the first time, but that doesn't mean you quit; it means you've got a chance to start over again. You can either take it as a lesson or say, "I quit. I'm not trying that any more."

I guess it's a matter of how badly you want what you desire. Things may not turn out exactly as you wanted, but that doesn't mean that you don't do it again. If my wife is baking a cake and one falls or turns out looking pitiful, she doesn't say, "I'll never bake another cake." She may determine that the oven was too hot or not hot enough or that she put in too much or too little water. By experimentation and trial, she improves each time, and she can use what she learned from the past it to do it again or to avoid doing what went wrong, until she gets better at it.

As learners, we learn. We should get feedback; we should learn from what worked and what didn't, but we can also study. We don't live long enough to make all the mistakes. That's why we read books on people overcoming adversity and things that went wrong in their lives, even including the kids who inherited lots of money and led a disastrous life. We'll never know all the answers, but learning is a lifelong process.

The older you get, the more you realize what you don't know. To me it's an absolutely wonderful world. You can concentrate on the negatives: people doing things that are very dramatic, committing crimes, and these things make the papers. We also have thousands and thousands of people out there doing good, even though that doesn't make the papers. Yet these people are happy in knowing that they made a difference to some young person's life or in a community.

We're never going to give up because some people go astray or make mistakes. We don't say, "Well, ain't no point in trying." You will teach some kids who will still end up on drugs. That doesn't mean you're going to forsake all the young people out there. After all, we don't hear much about the ones that do good; we hear about the ones that go astray.

We'll never have 100 percent efficiency, but the guy that bats 3 for 10—.300—will make the majors. Another guys bats 2 for 10—.200. This doesn't seem like a lot of difference, but the second guy goes nowhere. He will have to stay in the minor leagues and then go out and get a job doing something else. As Hill said, the slight differences are big, especially when applied over time.

Resources

In conclusion, let me talk about some resources. If you want to learn more about our certification course for teaching our methods, if you want to buy some of the books that I've been talking about, or if you want to sign up for our free weekly newsletter, visit our website: naphill.org.

We also carry a thought for the day, and we get an unbelievable number of compliments on it. We've been doing it for many years. We do a newsletter every Friday: you sign up, and it's free.

Of course, we list our books, we list upcoming books, and we highlight some books. You can simply click on the title of the book, and the link will take you to Amazon. When you buy a book this way, inside it's got the copyright for Napoleon Hill Foundation. You'll know that the money that's made on the books is going to a worthwhile cause, because we do many things that have no money return.

For example, we're probably one of the leading suppliers of material to the prisons. Practically every day, we get letters from people in prison. They've read *Think and Grow Rich* or another book and want to get a book.

There was one kid who was in prison for murder. I sent him books for probably fifteen years. He got his BS degree and his MBA while in prison. I wrote a letter to the parole board on his behalf. He was released, and he's working today.

We've got all kinds of stories. One of them is Bill Sands, who wrote a book called *My Shadow Ran Fast*. He was a young man, in his early twenties. His dad was a federal judge, and his mother was a socialite. Although he was an only child, they never saw him play Little League; they were too busy with their own lives. He thought, "Who cares about me?" So he got in with the wrong crowd. Although he never killed anybody, he got a long-term sentence to San Quentin. He read our books, and they changed his life. He was paroled, and he gave over three thousand speeches to high-school kids, warning them of the effects of drugs. He had been in trouble, but he straightened himself out, and he did a lot of good.

Never give up on anybody. As long as they're breathing, there's always a hope that they can change. Most of them want to, and they can see where they went wrong. If they do, they make tremendous examples for other people: "This is what caused me to get in trouble, and this is what I did to get out of it."

My Legacy

If someone were to ask me how I would like to be remembered, I would say that it was for trying to help other people, those who are less fortunate. I consider myself extremely lucky to be given this opportunity. There are 350 million people in this country, and *I'm* CEO of the Napoleon Hill Foundation? I probably don't deserve it.

I'm blessed beyond measure for what I've had in my life. When I was going to school, I didn't have a Corvette. My first vehicle was a '36 Ford, but I earned the money for it, and I was just as happy with it as if you had given me a Cadillac convertible, because I'd earned it.

I hope I will be discussed in terms of what I did for others.

I would rather have kids get up and go to school knowing that someone said, "It will be a lot better," than have people say I was a bank president or wonder how many stocks I owned. To know that you made a difference in somebody else's life is worth a million times as much as any material accumulation. The money was simply a product of what I was doing that I love to do.

I don't mean to boast, but I'm also president of the Foundation Board, which is the money-raising arm of the College.

Recently *U.S. News and World Report* said our students graduated with the second-lowest debt load of any four-year college in the United States. Quite an accomplishment, because we're a little college with two thousand students.

Anyway, there's enjoyment in trying to make a difference in somebody else's life. As a mentor of mine once said, "People send their money where their heart is." And Winston Churchill said, "We make a living by what we get; we make a life by what we give." It's nice to have things to make us happy, but to make a difference in somebody else's life, whether it's large or small, to me is the greatest satisfaction of all.

NINE

Favorite Quotes
from Napoleon Hill

Any definite purpose that is deliberately fixed in the
mind and held there, with the determination to realize
it, finally saturates the entire subconscious mind until
it automatically influences the physical action of the
body toward the attainment of that purpose.

. . . .

This subconscious mind may be likened to a magnet, and
when it has been vitalized and thoroughly saturated with
any definite purpose, it has a decided tendency to attract
all that is necessary for the fulfillment of that purpose.

. . . .

The development of self-confidence starts with the elimination of this demon called fear, which sits up on a man's shoulder and whispers into his ear, "You can't do it. You are afraid to try. You're afraid of public opinion. You are afraid that you will fail. You are afraid that you have not the ability."

. . . .

The human mind . . . may be likened to an electric battery; it may be positive or it may be negative. Self-confidence is the quality with which the mind is recharged and made positive.

. . . .

Success is the knowledge with which one may get all that he needs without violating the rights of his fellow men, or compromising with his own conscience.

. . . .

The law of harmonious attraction translates all thoughts into their kindred material counterparts. This great truth explains why the majority of people experience unhappiness and poverty throughout their lives. They allow their minds to fear unhappiness and poverty, and their dominating thoughts are on these circumstances. The law of harmonious attraction takes over and brings them that which they expect.

. . . .

When you deliver the best service of which you are capable, striving each time to excel all your previous

efforts, you are making use of the highest form of
education. Therefore, when you render more service
and better service than that for which you are paid, you
are profiting by the effort more than anyone else.

. . . .

There is a great power of attraction back of the person
who has a positive character, and this power expresses
itself through unseen as well as the visible sources. The
moment you come within speaking distance of such a
person, even though not a word is spoken, the influence
of the unseen power within makes itself felt.

. . . .

There is a difference between wishing for a thing
and being ready to receive it. No one is ready for a
thing until he believes he can acquire it.

. . . .

The state of mind must be belief,
not mere hope or wish.

. . . .

Open-mindedness is essential for belief. Closed
minds do not inspire faith, courage, and belief.

. . . .

All thoughts which have been emotionalized,
given feeling, and mixed with faith, begin
immediately to translate themselves into their
physical equivalent or counterpart.

. . . .

DON GREEN WITH A CUTOUT OF HIS MENTOR, NAPOLEON HILL

Afterword

The following two speeches are reprinted courtesy of Sound Wisdom, from the book *Napoleon Hill's Greatest Speeches*. They are from the archives and were previously never published. I am also including Dr. J. B. Hill's foreword from that title.

The first is "The End of the Rainbow: 1922 Commencement Address at Salem College." It is very historical as it inspired Hill to write *Think and Grow Rich*. It is preceded by Don Green's original introduction.

The other speech is "The Five Essentials of Success: 1957 Baccalaureate Sermon at Salem College." The introduction for this speech is written by Don Green and Dr. J. B. Hill.

Foreword to *Napoleon Hill's Greatest Speeches*

by Dr. J. B. Hill

Napoleon Hill rarely used more than a single page of notes to deliver his speeches. While many of these notes still exist, little of what he actually said has survived. It took me many years to locate one of my grandfather's speeches in print. Finding one was more than just exhilarating to me; it was miraculous.

The document I found was a transcript of a commencement address that Napoleon gave at Salem College (now Salem International University) in 1922. It had been published in a local newspaper under the title "The End of the Rainbow." A copy was preserved on microfilm in the archives of Salem College. When printed, it required magnification to read, and the text was so faded that it took more than a day to recover, which I did by dictating it one word at a time to my wife.

Napoleon wrote many times that adversity should be viewed as a blessing in disguise. In the 1922 commencement address, Napoleon shows how his many business failures were actually turning points that led him to greater opportunities. Each failure had therefore been a blessing.

He attributes his success following failure to the habit of performing more and better service than he was being paid for. This trait was the precursor of two of his principles of success: *Learning from Adversity and Defeat* and *Going the Extra Mile.*

Napoleon delivered the 1922 speech in Salem, West Virginia, not far from his wife Florence's family home in Lumberport. Although he was the editor and publisher of *Napoleon Hill's Magazine* at the time and a success by every measure, he had much to prove to family. Ten business failures in a dozen years had soured family attitudes toward him. So, the commencement address was Napoleon's opportunity to be applauded before his wife's friends and family, and in this, he succeeded. His delivery rhythm was mesmerizing to his audience. He used his personal history of failures to demonstrate how he was able to overcome adversity. The speech was touted to be the greatest ever given in that part of the state. When it ended, amid resounding applause, Napoleon stood before family, vindicated.

I sent a copy of the speech to Don Green, who is executive director of the Napoleon Hill Foundation. Don immediately saw the potential for a book and began searching through the archives of the foundation for additional material. Over several years, he discovered a few more speeches and a number of articles that he collated for this book.

One of the articles, "This Changing World," had been discovered behind the mantel of a fireplace in Napoleon's boyhood home. It was written during the Great Depression, probably near the end of 1930.

When the Depression struck, Napoleon was living with family who provided him with secure employment. However, to him, his acceptance of that security meant that he had failed. So, in March 1931, Hill did exactly what he needed to do—and perhaps exactly what he shouldn't have done: he quit his job and left for Washington, DC.

By this time, Napoleon's list of failed business ventures was impressive. His decision to try once more to succeed on his own must have been founded in faith—he certainly possessed little else. The article retrieved from behind the mantel provides an understanding of that faith and insight into why Napoleon later left family and security for Washington, DC, during a worldwide depression. "This Changing World" answers many persistent questions concerning Napoleon's spiritual views.

Don also located two copies of one of Napoleon's earliest speeches, "What I Learned from Analyzing Ten Thousand People." One had been stored in the Napoleon Hill Foundation archives, and the other had been published in the February 1918 issue of *Modern Methods*. Napoleon wrote the speech while serving as dean of the George Washington Institute of

Advertising (now the Bryant & Stratton Business College of Chicago), where he later became president and director of the Salesmanship and Advertising Department.

In this speech, Napoleon talks about the five "requisites" for success: self-confidence, enthusiasm, concentration, a working plan, and the habit of performing more and better services than paid for. It reveals Napoleon's early thinking about three of what would become some of his principles of success: *Enthusiasm, Controlled Attention*, and *Going the Extra Mile*. Later he grouped the requisite of "self-confidence" under the heading of *Enthusiasm*, and "a working plan" became part of the process of achieving a *Definite Major Purpose*. Although Napoleon understood the importance of Andrew Carnegie's "Master Mind" idea, he did not mention it in this speech. I suspect it just wasn't pertinent for an audience of salesmen who tend toward having individual pathways to success.

At the end of 1952, Napoleon left his wife, Annie Lou, in California for a year while he worked with W. Clement Stone on a number of projects. For several months he and Stone toured together on the lecture circuit, with Stone often introducing Napoleon as a keynote speaker.

Don discovered a recording of one of these keynotes titled "Maker of Miracle Men" and had it transcribed for this book. It is perhaps the most interesting of his finds because it faithfully depicts Napoleon in extemporaneous mode. Napoleon's wit and spellbinding oratory are palpable in the prose.

By the middle of the 1950s, Napoleon was well known nationally as a speaker. His lectures had spread to radio and television, and Pacific International University had awarded him an honorary doctor of literature degree. In 1957, Salem College invited him back to give a baccalaureate sermon and to receive a second honorary doctorate.

By this time, Napoleon's ideas about success had matured until they had morphed into concrete principles. Instead of lecturing about the five *requisites* for success, he covers in his baccalaureate sermon, titled "The Five Essentials of Success," the five most important *principles* of success. Like the 1922 commencement speech, it too was applauded wildly by his audience.

It is interesting to note that after thirty-five years of thought, only *Going the Extra Mile* among the original five 1922 requisites for success remained essential in Napoleon's mind. The other requisites had been replaced by four essential principles: *Master Mind*, *Definiteness of Purpose*, *Self-Discipline*, and *Applied Faith*.

While each of the speeches and articles in this collection stands alone, together they show how Napoleon's ideas evolved as his thought matured and coalesced into a comprehensive philosophy of success. The aggregated material truly has greater significance than its parts.

In 1922, Napoleon Hill was invited to give the commencement address at Salem College in Salem, West Virginia.
The school was founded in 1888 as a liberal arts, teacher
education, and nursing college. Titled "The End of the
Rainbow," the commencement address was the most
influential speech that Hill ever gave.

When Hill delivered the speech in 1922, he was thirty-
nine years old and had many years' experience in writing
and speaking, but he was still several years away from
publishing his first book. He was passionately focused on
his speechmaking and lectured anywhere he could get an
audience. As Hill became better known, especially after
he became a published author, his lectures were in great
demand. In the archives of the Napoleon Hill Foundation
are recorded the data of eighty-nine speeches he gave
throughout the country—all in just one year.

The 1922 speech Hill gave at Salem College inspired a
letter he received years later from a member of Congress,
Jennings Randolph. Hill was to mention this letter in the
introduction to his 1937 book *Think and Grow Rich*, and

to print Randolph's inspirational letter. Randolph won his seat in Congress in 1932, the same year that Franklin D. Roosevelt was elected president of the United States.

Randolph introduced Hill to Roosevelt, and Hill became an unpaid advisor to the president during the Great Depression. Written correspondence from the White House is contained in the Napoleon Hill Foundation's archives.

Randolph would later become a US Senator and a trustee of the Napoleon Hill Foundation. He died in 1998 and was the last member of Congress to have served in the beginning of the Franklin D. Roosevelt Administration.

The recovery of the newspaper account of the speech is the result of the diligent work of Dr. J. B. Hill, grandson of Napoleon Hill, who was able to obtain the speech from microfilm, and Dr. J. B. Hill's wife, Nancy, who retyped it. The following is that speech.

—Don Green

The End of the Rainbow
1922 Commencement Address at Salem College

by Napoleon Hill

There is a legend as old as the human race that tells us that a pot of gold can be found at the end of a rainbow. This fairy tale, which grips the imaginative child's mind, may have something to do with the present tendency of the human race to look for the easy way to find riches. For nearly twenty years I sought the end of my rainbow that I might claim that pot of gold. My struggle in search of the evasive rainbow's end was ceaseless. It carried me up the mountainside of failure and down the hillsides of despair, luring me on and on in search of the phantom pot of gold.

I was sitting before a fire one night discussing with older people the question of unrest upon the part of laboring men.

The labor union movement had just begun to make itself felt in that part of the country where I then lived, and the tactics used by the labor organizers impressed me as being too revolutionary and obstructive ever to bring permanent success. One of the men who sat before that fireside with me made a comment that proved to be one of the best pieces of advice that I have ever followed. He reached over and firmly grasped me by the shoulders, looked me squarely in the eyes, and said: "Why, you are a bright boy, and if you will give yourself an education, you will make your mark in this world."*

The first concrete result of that remark caused me to enroll in a local business college, a step which I am dutybound to admit proved to be one of the most helpful that I ever took because I got my first fleeting glimpse in business college of what one might call a fair sense of proportions.† After completing business college, I obtained a position as a stenographer and bookkeeper and worked in this capacity for several years.‡

As a result of this idea of performing more service and better service than paid for, which I had learned in business college, I advanced rapidly and always succeeded in filling positions of responsibility far in advance of my years, with salary proportionate.

---

* This had to be in 1902 when Hill was about nineteen years old. Apparently, he worked briefly as a coal miner before attending business college.

† The idea of performing more service and better service than paid for later became the principle *Going the Extra Mile*.

‡ This was during the time that Hill worked for Rufus Ayers.

I saved money and soon had a bank account amounting to several thousand dollars. I was rapidly advancing toward my rainbow's end.

My reputation spread rapidly and I found competitive bidders for my services. I was in demand, not because of what I knew, which was little enough, but because of my willingness to make the best use of what little I did know. This spirit of willingness proved to be the most powerful and strategic principle I ever learned.

The tides of fate blew me southward and I became sales manager for a large lumber manufacturing concern. I knew nothing about lumber and I knew nothing about sales management, but I had learned that it was well to render better service and more of it than I was paid for; and with this principle as the dominant spirit, I tackled my job with the determination to find out all I could about selling lumber.

I made a good record. My salary was increased twice during the year and my bank account was growing bigger and bigger. I did so well in managing the sales of my employer's lumber that he organized a new lumber company and took me into partnership with him.

I could see myself growing nearer and nearer to the rainbow's end. Money and success poured in to me from every direction, all of which fixed my attention steadfastly on the pot of gold that I could plainly see just ahead of me. Up to this time it did not occur to me that success could consist of anything except gold!

The Unseen Hand

The "Unseen Hand" allowed me to strut around under the influence of my vanity until I had begun to feel my importance. In the light of more sober years and a more accurate interpretation of human events I now wonder if the "Unseen Hand" does not purposely permit us foolish human beings to parade before our own mirror of vanity until we see how vulgar we are and stop it.

At any rate, I seemed to have a clear track ahead; there was coal in the bunker, water in the tank, my hand was on the throttle and I opened it wide. Fate was awaiting me just around the bend with a stuffed club, and it wasn't stuffed with cotton. And I did not see the impending crash until it came.

Like a stroke of lightning out of the clear blue sky, an economic collapse and panic crashed down on me. Overnight it swept away every dollar that I had. The man with whom I was in business withdrew, panic-stricken but without loss, and left me with nothing but the empty shell of a company that owned nothing except a good reputation. I could have bought a hundred thousand dollars of lumber on that reputation.

A crooked lawyer saw a chance to cash in on that reputation and what was left of the lumber company on my hands. He and a group of other men purchased the company and continued to operate it. I learned later that they bought every dollar worth of lumber that they could get, resold it, and pocketed the proceeds without paying for it. Thus, I had been the innocent means of helping them defraud their creditors, who learned when it was too late that I was in no way connected with the company.

It required an economic collapse and the next failure that it brought to me to divert and redirect my efforts from the lumber business to the study of law. Nothing on earth but failure, or what I then called failure, could have brought about that result. Thus, a turning point of my life was ushered in on the wings of failure. There is a great lesson in every failure whether we know what it is or not.*

When I entered law school, it was with the firm belief that I would emerge doubly prepared to catch up with the end of the rainbow and claim my pot of gold. I still had no higher aspiration than that of accumulating money; yet, the very thing that I worshiped most seemed to be the most elusive thing on earth, for it was always evading me, always in sight, but always just out of reach.

I attended law school at night and worked as an automobile salesman during the day. My sales experience in the lumber business was turned to good advantage. I prospered rapidly, doing so well from the habit of performing more and better service than paid for that the opportunity came to open a school to train ordinary machinists in automotive assembly and repair work. This school prospered until it was paying me a large monthly salary. Again I had my rainbow's end in sight. Again

---

* This shows Hill's early thinking about the positive effects of failure.

I knew that I had at last found my niche in the world's work. Again I knew that nothing could swerve me from my course or cause me to divert my attention.

My banker saw me prospering. He extended me credit for expansion. He encouraged me to invest in outside lines of business. He appeared to me to be one of the finest men in the world. He loaned me many thousands of dollars on my signature, without endorsement.

My banker loaned me money until I was hopelessly in his debt and then he took over my business. It all happened so suddenly that it dazed me. I didn't think such a thing possible. You see, I still had much to learn about the ways of men, especially the kind of man that unfortunately my banker turned out to be—a type which, in justice to the business of banking, I ought to say is rare.

This failure was one of the greatest blessings that ever was bestowed upon me.

From a man of affairs earning a good income, owner of half a dozen automobiles and much other junk which I didn't need, I was reduced to poverty. The rainbow's end disappeared, and it was many years before I learned that this failure was one of the greatest blessings that ever was bestowed upon me because it forced me out of a business which in no way helped me develop the human side and diverted my efforts into a channel that brought me an experience that I greatly needed.

I think it is worthy of note to state here that I went back to Washington, DC, a few years after the event and out of curiosity visited the old bank where I once had a liberal line of credit, expecting, of course, to find it still in operation. To my great surprise I found that the bank had gone out of business, and my erstwhile banker had been reduced to penury and want. I met him on the street, practically penniless. With eyes red and swollen, he aroused in me a questioning attitude, and I wondered for the first time in my life if one might find any other thing of value except money at the rainbow's end.

Because I was my wife's husband and her people had influence, I secured an appointment as assistant to the chief counsel for a family-owned business. My salary was greatly out of proportion to the wages that the company usually paid beginners, and still further out of proportion to what I was worth; but pull is pull, and I was there because I was there.

It turned out that what I lacked in legal ability, I supplied through that one sound, fundamental principle that I had learned in business college—namely, to render more service and better service than paid for, whenever possible.

I was holding my position without any difficulty. I practically had a berth for life if I cared to keep it. One day, I did what my close personal friends and relatives said was a very foolish thing: I quit my job abruptly.

When pressed for a reason, I gave what seemed to me to be a very sound one, but I had trouble convincing the family circle that I had acted wisely, and still greater difficulty convincing a few of my friends that I was perfectly rational in mind. I quit that job because I found the work too easy and demanding too little effort and I found myself drifting.*

This move proved to be an important turning point in my life, although it was followed by ten years of effort that brought almost every grief that the human heart could experience. I quit my job in the legal field, where I was getting along well, living among friends and relatives with what they believed to be a bright and unusually promising future, and I moved to Chicago.

I selected Chicago because I believed it to be the most competitive place in the world. I felt that if I could go to Chicago and gain recognition along any legitimate line, I would prove to myself that I had the material in me that might, some day, develop into real ability.

In Chicago, I secured the position of advertising manager.† I knew next to nothing about advertising, but my previous experience as a salesman came to my rescue, and my old friend, the habit of performing more services than paid for, gave me a fair balance on the credit side of the ledger.

The first year I flourished. I was coming back by leaps and bounds. Gradually, the rainbow began to circle around me, and I saw once more that shining pot of gold almost within reach. I believe it of importance to recall the fact that my standard of success was always measured in terms of dollars and my rain-

---

* Hill felt that "drifting" was one of the greatest reasons for failure in life.

† Hill's first job in Chicago was as advertising manager for LaSalle.

bow's end promised nothing but a pot of gold. Up to this point, if I thought that anything except gold might be found at the end of the rainbow, that thought was momentary and quickly vanished. History is full of evidence that a feast usually precedes a fall. I was having my feast but never thought of the fall. I suspect that no one ever anticipates the fall until it comes, but come it will, unless one's fundamental guiding principles are sound.

I made a good record as an advertising manager. The president of the company was attracted by my work and later helped organize the Betsy Ross Candy Company, and I became its president, thus beginning the next most important turning point of my life and the prelude to another failure.*

The business began to expand until we had a chain of stores in many different cities.† Again I saw my rainbow's end almost within reach. I knew that I had at last found the business in which I wanted to remain for life, and I frankly admit that our business was fashioned after that of another candy company whose western manager was my personal friend. His overwhelming success was the main factor in causing me to enter the candy business.

Everything went smoothly for a time, until my business associate and a third man whom we later took into the business conceived the notion to gain control of my interests without pay-

---

* The candy recipes had been passed down from Hill's mother, Sara Blair. His first wife, Florence, was skilled in making these candies.

† Per Hill's biography, *Lifetime of Riches*, these cities were Chicago, Baltimore, Indianapolis, Milwaukee, and Cleveland.

ing for it, a mistake that men never seem to understand that they are making until it is too late and they have paid the price of their folly.

The Plan Worked

The plan worked, but I balked more stiffly than they had anticipated; therefore, to gently urge me along toward the grand exit, they had me arrested on a false charge and offered to settle out of court if I would turn over my interest in the company.

I refused and insisted on going to trial. When the time arrived for court, no one was present to prosecute. We insisted on prosecution and requested the court to summon the complaining witness and make him prosecute, which was done.

The judge, the Honorable Arnold Heap, stopped the proceedings and threw the case out of court before it had gone very far, with the statement that "this is one of the most flagrant cases of attempted coercion that has ever come before me."

To protect my reputation I brought suit for fifty thousand dollars in damages. The case was tried five years later and I secured a heavy judgment in the Superior Court of Chicago. The suit was a "tort action," meaning that it claimed damages for the libelous injury to my reputation.

But I suspect that another and much more exacting law than that under which tort actions may be brought was operating during those five years because one of the parties—the one who originated the scheme to have me arrested as part of the plan to force my interests in the business away from me—was serving a term in the federal penitentiary before my action against him was tried, and for a crime separate and apart from the one he had committed against me. The other party had fallen from a high station in life to poverty and disgrace.

My judgment stands in the records of the Superior Court of Chicago as silent evidence of the vindication of my character and as evidence of something far more important than mere vindication; namely, that the "Unseen Hand" which guides the destiny of all who earnestly seek truth had eliminated from my nature all desire for my pound of flesh. My judgment against my transducers was not collected, and it never will be!

At least, I will never collect it, because I suspect that it has been paid many times over in blood and remorse and regret and failure visited upon those who would have destroyed my character for personal gain.

This was one of the greatest single blessings that ever came to me because it taught me to forgive! It taught me also that the law of compensation is always in operation and that "Whatsoever a man soweth, that shall he also reap."* It blotted out of my nature the last lingering thought of seeking personal revenge at any time under any circumstances. It taught me that time is the friend of all who are right and the mortal enemy of all who are unjust and destructive in their

---

* The law of compensation may be "just rewards"!

efforts. It brought me nearer to a full understanding of the Master when he said, "Forgive them Father for they know not what they do."

Teaching

We now come to another venture that probably brought me nearer the rainbow's end than any of the others because it placed me in a position where I found it necessary to bring all the knowledge that I had acquired up to that time, concerning every subject with which I was familiar, and gave me opportunity for self-expression and personal development such as rarely comes to a man so early in life.

I turned my efforts toward teaching advertising and salesmanship.*

Some wise philosopher has said that we never learn much until we start trying to teach others. My experience as a teacher proved that this is true. My school prospered from the start. I had a resident school and a correspondent school through which I was teaching students in nearly every English-speaking country.

In spite of the ravages of war, my school was growing by leaps and bounds, and I saw the end of my rainbow drawing nearer and nearer. I was so close that I could almost reach out and touch the pot of gold.

---

* This school was called the George Washington Institute of Advertising.

As a result of the record that I was making and the recognition I was gaining, I attracted the attention of the head of
a corporation, who employed me for three weeks out of each
month at a salary of $105,200 a year—considerably more than
the president of the United States receives.

In less than six months, I built up one of the most efficient
working forces in America and increased the assets of the company to a point where it was offered twenty million dollars more
for its business than it was worth when I started.

Candidly, had you been in my place, would you not have felt
justified in saying that you found your rainbow's end? Would
you have felt justified in saying that you had attained success?

I thought I had, but I had one of the rudest shocks of all
awaiting me, due partly to the dishonesty of the head of the corporation for whom I was working, but more directly, I suspect,
to a deeper and more significant cause concerning which fate
seemed to have decreed that I should learn something.

One hundred thousand dollars of my salary was condi-
tional upon my remaining as the directing head of staff for a
period of one year. In less than half that time, I began to see
that I was pyramiding power and placing it in the hands of a
man who was growing power-drunk. I began to see that ruin
awaited him just around the corner. This discovery brought
me much grief.

Morally, I was responsible for several million dollars of capital that I had induced the American people to invest in this
corporation. Legally, of course, I was in no way responsible.

I finally brought this matter to a head, delivering an ultimatum to the head of the corporation to safeguard the funds of the company under a board of financial control or else accept my resignation. He laughed at the suggestion because he thought I would not break my contract and thereby lose one hundred thousand dollars. Perhaps I would not have done so had it not been for the moral responsibility that I felt on behalf of the thousands of investors. I resigned and the company passed into the hands of receivership, and therefore I did all I could to protect it against the mismanagement of a money-mad young man, a bit of satisfaction that brought me much ridicule and cost me one hundred thousand dollars.

For the moment my rainbow's end seemed vague and somewhat distant. There were moments when I wondered what caused me to make a fool of myself and throw away a fortune just to protect those who never would even know that I had made sacrifices for them.

In my climax, I will tabulate the sum total of all that I have learned from each of the important failures and mileposts of my life, but first let me describe the last of those failures. To do so, I must go back to that eventful day—November 11, 1918. That was Armistice Day, as everyone knows. Like most other people, I became as drunk with enthusiasm and joy as any man ever did on wine.

I was practically penniless, as the war had destroyed my business, and I had turned my efforts to war work; but I was happy to know that the slaughter was over and reason was about to spread its beneficial wings over the earth once more. The war had swept away my school, from which my income would have amounted to over fifteen thousand dollars a year had our students not been drafted for war and had I not felt it my own duty to turn my efforts to helping my country in its time of need. I stood as far away from my rainbow's end as I did on that eventful day more than twenty years previously when I looked into the drift mouth of a coal mine where I was employed as a laborer, and thought of that statement that a kindly old gentleman had made to me the night before, but realized that a yawning chasm stood between me and any accomplishment other than a laborer in the mines.

Happy Again

But I was happy again! Again that tramp thought entered my consciousness and prompted me to ask myself if I had not been searching for the wrong sort of reward at my rainbow's end. I sat down to my typewriter with nothing particular in mind. To my astonishment, my hands began to play a regular symphony upon the keys of the typewriter. I had never written so rapidly or easily before. I did not think of what I was writing—I just wrote and wrote and kept on writing.

When I was through, I had five pages of manuscript, and as near as I have been able to determine, that manuscript was written without any organized thoughts on my part. It was an editorial out of which my first magazine, Napoleon Hill's Golden

Rule Magazine, was born. I took this editorial to a wealthy man and read it to him. Before I had read the last line, he had promised to finance my magazine. It was in this somewhat dramatic manner that a desire that had lain dormant in my mind for nearly twenty years began to express itself. It was the same idea that I had in mind when I made the statement that caused that old gentleman to lay his hand on my shoulder and make that fortunate remark twenty years previously, which had at its foundation the thought that the Golden Rule ought to be the guiding spirit in all human relationships.

All my life I had wanted to become a newspaper editor. More than twenty years ago, when I was a very small boy, I used to kick the press for my father, who published a small newspaper, and I grew to love the smell of printer's ink.

The important thing to which I would direct your attention is the fact that I found my proper niche in the world's work and I was very happy in it. Strangely enough, I entered upon this work, which constituted my last lap in the long, long trail over which I had traveled in search of my rainbow's end, with never a thought of finding a pot of gold.

The magazine prospered from the beginning. In less than six months, it was being read in every English-speaking country in the world. It has brought me recognition from all parts of the world, which resulted in a public speaking tour in 1920 covering every large city in America.

Up to now, I had made about as many enemies as I had friends. Now a strange thing has happened: beginning with my initial editorial work, I commenced to make friends by the thousands until today upwards of one hundred thousand people stand squarely back of me because they believe in me and my message.

What brought about this change?

If you understand the law of attraction, you can answer this because you know that like attracts like and that a man will attract friends or foes according to the nature of the thoughts that dominate his mind. One cannot take a belligerent attitude toward life and expect to make friends. When I commenced to preach the Golden Rule in my first magazine, I started to live it as near as I could.

There is a big difference between merely believing in the Golden Rule and actually practicing it in overt acts, a truth I learned when I began my first magazine. This realization brought me abruptly into an understanding of a principle that now permeates every thought that finds a permanent lodging place in my mind and dominates every act I perform as nearly as humanly possible, and that thought is none other than the one laid down by the Master in his Sermon on the Mount when he admonished us to "do unto others as we would have others do unto us."

During these past three years since, I have been sending out Golden Rule thought vibrations to hundreds of thousands of people. These thought waves have multiplied themselves in the rebound and have brought back to me floods of goodwill from those whom my message reached.

I was rapidly approaching my rainbow's end for the seventh and last time. Every avenue of failure seemed closed. My enemies had been slowly transformed into friends and I was making new friends by the thousands. But there was a final test to undergo.

As I have stated, I was approaching the end of my rainbow with the firm belief that nothing on earth could stop me from attaining it and obtaining my pot of gold and everything else that a successful searcher for that great reward might expect.

Like a stroke of lightning out of the clear sky, I received a shock!

The impossible had happened. My first magazine, Napoleon Hill's Golden Rule Magazine, was not only snatched out of my hand overnight, but its influence that I had built up was temporarily turned as a weapon against me.

Again, man had failed me, and I thought unkind thoughts about man. It was a savage blow to me when I awoke to the realization that there was no truth to the Golden Rule that I had been preaching to thousands of people through the pages of my magazine and in person and had been doing my level best to live as well.

This was the supreme moment of testing.

Had my experience proved my most beloved principle to be false and nothing more than a snare with which to trip the untutored, or was I about to learn a great lesson which would establish the truth and soundness of those principles for the remainder of my life and perhaps throughout eternity?

These were the questions that pressed upon me.

I did not answer them quickly; I could not. I was so stunned that I had to stop and catch my breath. I had been preaching that one could not steal another man's ideas, or plans, or goods and wares and still prosper. My experience seemed to give the lie to all I had ever written or spoken along this line because the men who stole the child of my heart and brain seemed not only to be prospering with it, but they had actually used it as a means of stopping me from carrying out my plans for worldwide service in the interest of the human race.

Months passed by, and I was unable to turn a wheel. I had been deposed, my magazine had been taken away from me, and my friends seemed to look upon me as a sort of fallen Richard the Lionheart. Some said I would come back stronger and bigger for the experience. Others said I was through. Thus the remarks came and went, but I stood looking on in wonderment, feeling much the same as a person feels who is undergoing a nightmare and so cannot awaken or move as much as a finger.

Literally I was experiencing a wide-awake nightmare that seemed to hold me firmly within its grasp. My courage was gone. My faith in humanity was all but gone. My love for humanity was weakening. Slowly but surely I was reversing my opinion concerning the highest and best ideals that I had been building for more than a score of years. The passing weeks seemed like an eternity. The days seemed like a whole lifetime.

One day the atmosphere began to clear.

Some cloudy atmospheres usually do clear away. Time is a wonderful healer of wounds. Time cures nearly everything that is sick or ignorant, and most of us are both at times.

Time cures nearly everything that is sick or ignorant, and most of us are both at times.

During the seventh and greatest failure of my life, I was reduced to greater poverty than any I had ever known before. From a well-furnished home, I was reduced practically over-night to a one-room apartment. Coming as this blow did, just as I was about to lay hold of the pot of gold at my rainbow's end, it cut a deep and ugly wound in my heart. During this brief testing spell, I was made to kneel in the very dust of poverty and eat the crust of all my past follies. When I had all but given up, the clouds of darkness began to float away as rapidly as they had come.

I stood face to face with one of the most trying tests that ever came to me. Perhaps no human being ever was more severely tried than I was—at least that was the way I felt about it at the time.

The postman had delivered my scant collection of mail. As I opened it, I was watching the pale red sun as it had all but disap-peared over the western horizon. To me it was symbolic of that which was about to happen to me, for I saw my sun of hope also setting in the west. I opened the envelope on top, and as I did so, a certificate of deposit fluttered to the floor and fell face upward.

It was for twenty-five thousand dollars. For a whole minute I stood with my eyes glued to that bit of paper, wondering if I were not dreaming. I walked over closer to it, picked it up, and read the letter accompanying it.

That money was mine! I could draw it out of the bank at will. Only two slight strings were attached to it, but these strings made it necessary to obligate myself morally to turn my back on everything that I had been preaching about, placing the interest of the people above those of any individual.

The supreme moment of testing had come. Would I accept that money which was ample capital with which to publish my magazine or would I return it and carry on a little longer? These were the first questions that claimed my attention.

Then I heard the ringing of a bell in the region of my heart. This time its sound was more direct. It caused the blood to tingle through my body. With the ringing of the bell came the most direct command that ever registered itself in my consciousness, and that command was accompanied by a chemical change in my brain such as I had never experienced before. It was a positive, startling command, and it brought a message that I could not misunderstand.

Without promise of a reward, it made me return that twenty-five thousand dollars.

I hesitated. That bell kept on ringing. My feet seemed glued to the spot. I could not move out of my tracks. Then I reached my decision. I decided to heed that prompting, which no one but a fool could have mistaken.

The instant I reached this conclusion, I looked, and in the approaching twilight, I saw the rainbow's end. I had at last caught up with it. I saw no pot of gold except the one I was about to send back to the source from which it came, but I found something more precious than all the gold in the world, as I heard a voice that reached me, not through my ears, but through my heart.

And it said: "Standeth God within the shadow of every failure."

The end of my rainbow brought me the triumph of principle over gold. It gave me a closer communion with the great "Unseen Force" of this universe and new determination to plant the seed of the Golden Rule philosophically in the hearts of millions of other weary travelers who are seeking the end of their rainbow.

---

*The end of my rainbow brought me
the triumph of principle over gold.*

In the July 1921 issue of Napoleon Hill's Magazine, my secretary tells of one of the most dramatic events that followed closely upon my decision not to accept financial help from sources that would in any extent whatsoever control my pen. That incident is only one, each constituting sufficient evidence to convince all but fools that the Golden Rule really works, that the law of compensation is in operation, and that "Whatsoever a man soweth, that shall he also reap."

Not alone did I get all the capital necessary to carry Napoleon Hill's Magazine over the beginning period, during which its own revenues were insufficient to publish it, but what is of greater significance—the magazine is growing with rapidity heretofore unknown in the field of similar periodicals. The readers and the public generally have caught the spirit of the work we are doing and they have put the law of increasing returns into operation in our favor.

The Most Important Lessons

Now let me summarize the most important lessons I learned in my search for the rainbow's end. I will not try to mention all the lessons but only the most important ones. I will leave to your own imagination much that you can see without my recounting it here.

First and most important of all, in my search for the rainbow's end, I found God in every concrete, understandable, and satisfying manifestation, which is quite significant if I found nothing more. All my life I had been somewhat unsettled as to the exact nature of that "Unseen Hand" which directs the affairs of the universe, but my seven turning points on the rainbow trail of life brought me, at last, to a conclusion that satisfies. Whether my conclusion is right or wrong is not of much importance; the main thing is that it satisfies me.

The lessons of importance that I learned are these:

I learned that those whom we consider our enemies are in reality our friends. In the light of all that has happened, I would not begin to go back and undo a single one of these trying experiences with which I met because each one of them brought to me positive evidence of the soundness of the Golden Rule and the existence of the law of compensation, through which we claim our rewards for virtue and pay the penalties for our ignorance.

I learned that time is a friend of all who base their thoughts and actions on truth and justice and that it is the mortal enemy of all who fail to do so, even though the penalty of the reward is often slow in arriving where it is due.

I learned that the only pot of gold worth striving for is that which comes from the satisfaction of knowing that one's efforts are bringing happiness to others.

One by one I have seen those who are unjust with me cut down by failure. I have lived to see every one of them reduced to failure far beyond anything that they planned against me. The banker whom I mentioned was reduced to poverty; the men who stole my interest in the Betsy Ross Candy Company and tried to destroy my reputation have come down to what looks like permanent failure, one of them living as a convict in a federal prison.

The man who defrauded me out of my one hundred thousand-dollar salary and whom I elevated to wealth and influence has been reduced to poverty and want. At every turn of the road that led finally to my rainbow's end I saw undisputable evidence to back the Golden Rule philosophy that I am now sending forth through organized effort to hundreds of thousands of people.

Lastly, I have learned to listen for the ringing of the bell that guides me when I come to the crossroads of doubt and hesitancy. I have learned to tap a heretofore unknown source from which I get my promptings when I wish to know which way to turn and what to do, and these promptings have never led me in the wrong direction. As I finish, I see on the walls of my study the portraits of great men whose lives I have tried to emulate. Among them is that immortal Lincoln, from whose rugged, careworn face I seem to see a smile emerging and from whose lips I can all but hear the magic words: "With charity to all and malice toward none." And deep down in my heart, I hear that mysterious bell ringing, and bellowing it comes once more as I close these lines with the greatest message that ever reached my consciousness: "Standeth God within the shadow of every failure."

When Napoleon Hill was asked to deliver the baccalaureate sermon on June 2, 1957, at Salem College, it
had been thirty-five years since he had delivered a commencement address to the 1922 graduating class at the
same college.

In *The Alumni Echoes*, the school paper of Salem
College, the headline read "Convocation Set Today." The
paper had the following to say about Dr. Hill:

Napoleon Hill, philosopher, author, and educator who
has taught more people how to achieve financial and
spiritual success in life than any other living person,
will deliver the baccalaureate address at 8:00 p.m. on
Sunday, June 2, in the Salem College auditorium.

During a personally exciting life, he developed the
"science of success," an exact study which laid down
the principles by which anyone can realize his material
goals no matter what ambitions they may be.

Mr. Hill has, moreover, been the confidant and
adviser to presidents, industrialists, and government

leaders including Franklin D. Roosevelt, Woodrow Wilson, Andrew Carnegie, and Henry Ford. In fact, it was Carnegie who first started him on the research that resulted in Mr. Hill's development of the "seventeen principles of success."

Literally millions of persons credit Mr. Hill with inspiring them to greater heights of fortune in life than they ever believed possible. More than that, he has furnished them with practical step-by-step methods for realizing their ambitions.

"What the human mind can conceive and believe, the human mind can achieve" is the core of Mr. Hill's philosophy.

"You can," he says, "be anything you want to be, if only you believe with sufficient conviction—and act in accordance with your faith."

It is estimated that sixty million people throughout the world have read and benefited from his most notable book, *Think and Grow Rich*, since it was published in 1937.

Napoleon Hill was born in Wise County, Virginia, on October 26, 1883, amidst "moonshiners, mountain stills, illiteracy, and deadly feuds." Although born in poverty, it was said he was given the unusual name of Napoleon in honor of his rich paternal great uncle.

With a view toward financing his further education, Mr. Hill launched a new project at the age of twenty-five. He began writing biographical articles about successful people for Senator Bob Taylor of Tennessee, publisher of an important periodical of the day.

Rep. Jennings Randolph, who credited Hill with helping him to achieve his own success as an executive of Capital Airlines, introduced Mr. Hill in 1933 to Franklin D. Roosevelt, and as a result, Hill became a presidential advisor. It was he who gave FDR the idea for his famous speech—*"We have nothing to fear but fear itself"*—which helped halt financial hysteria at the pit of the Depression.

Mr. Hill was interested in and helpful to Salem College long years ago and delivered the commencement address in 1922. He is the publisher of *Success Unlimited* magazine. He is also the author of many books on personal improvement, including *Think and Grow Rich*, which has sold more than sixty million copies and has been reprinted in the languages of other countries. One of his more recent volumes was *How to Raise Your Own Salary.*

Hill is married and has three adult sons. He and his wife live quietly in Glendale, California.

Much had happened in the life of Hill since 1922 when he addressed the twenty-five graduates including Jennings Randolph, who was to represent West Virginia in Congress. Mr. Randolph served for many years in the US Congress and became a friend to Hill and later served as trustee on the board of the Napoleon Hill Foundation.

At the 1957 address, Hill was awarded an honorary doctorate in literature.

—Don Green

The Five Essentials of Success
1957 Baccalaureate Sermon
at Salem College

by Napoleon Hill

The dictionary describes a baccalaureate as—and here I quote—"a farewell sermon to a graduating class at commencement."

What I have to say to you does not constitute a sermon, and it certainly isn't a farewell!

Actually, my message to you is one of greeting, for it's my great pleasure and honor to extend a hearty welcome as you leave the scholastic world and enter the business and professional world.

I sincerely hope that my oratorical powers are sufficient to make my message highly personal so that each of you young ladies and gentlemen feel that I am speaking directly to you. For it is on this personal note that I think you will derive the greatest benefit from what I have to say.

In other words, I hope that when I've finished, you won't feel like the woman who shook hands with her minister after church one Sunday and said: "That was a wonderful sermon! Everything said applies to somebody or other I know!"

Or I might cite the case of the clergyman who illustrated a point in his sermon by saying something about which of us grows best in sunlight and which of us must have shade.

"You know," the minister told his congregation, "that you plant roses in the sunlight. But if you want fuchsias to grow, they must be kept in a shady nook."

Afterwards, the minister's heart glowed when a woman grasped his hand and said: "Pastor, I'm so grateful for your splendid sermon!" But his gratification subsided when she went on to say: "You know, I never knew before just what was the matter with my fuchsias!"

I hope that each of you will learn how to plant certain seeds that will reap you a rich harvest of spiritual and material happiness.

I'm afraid that none of you will learn how to grow fuchsias from me today. But in a sense, my message *does* apply to gardening. For from my words I hope that each of you will learn how to plant certain seeds that, in years to come, will reap you a rich harvest of spiritual and material happiness. And if each of you learns just one little tip on how to cultivate the garden of life—like the lady with her fuchsias—I shall be satisfied.

On the other hand, I hope you won't go away feeling like the little girl who attended church for the first time. When the minister asked her how she liked the service, she replied: "Well, I thought the music was very nice—but your commercial was too long!"

Just thirty-five years ago this summer I stood on this same rostrum and addressed the graduating class of Salem College. That was in 1922. World War I had just ended. In that great conflict America had been the deciding factor in bringing victory to the Allies. Our country was just emerging as the greatest political and economic power on earth. Consequently, it took no great power of prophecy for me to draw a beautiful picture for the Salem College graduating class of 1922. I was able, at that time, to call the attention of the graduates to the abundance of opportunities for personal advancement in this nation. And I was able to predict accurately that our country was entering upon its greatest period of industrial and economic expansion in history. There were some things that—I'm glad to say—I could not foresee. One of these was the Great Depression of the thirties.

The other was World War II and the rise of Communism. It almost seems as though blessed Providence lifts the veil of the future a bit to let us forecast the good things ahead of us but mercifully withholds knowledge of forthcoming evil! It has been a great pleasure to me during these past thirty-five years to watch unfold many of the predictions I made on that summer's day in 1922. I must admit, however, that my wildest, most optimistic dreams on that day came nowhere near to depicting the glorious reality! No doubt there are in today's audience at least a few from the graduating class of 1922. And I'm certain that they will forgive me for failing then to foresee the stupendous advances that man would make in the fields of science and culture. For who—in 1922—could have predicted such things as nuclear energy, the tremendous growth of the aviation and electronics industries, or our conquest of distance and time? Why, if I had dared to predict in 1922 that man would fly two and three times the speed of sound, I feel certain that members of the faculty and the graduating class would have laughed me off the stage.

(Looking at the college president) Isn't that so?

There is a great lesson for you young people in all this. It's simply this: no matter how optimistic and hopeful my words sound today, no matter how I let my imagination roam, no matter how glowingly I describe the future, I cannot possibly hope to draw a full picture of the glorious achievements mankind will accomplish during the next thirty-five years!

At this point I'm reminded of the taxicab driver in Washington, DC, who drove a tourist past the Government Archives Building. On the building there is carved a motto that reads:

"What is Past is Prologue."

"What does the motto mean?" the visitor asked.

"Well," said the driver, "it means you ain't seen nothing yet!"

The things you are destined to see during your lifetime, the glorious accomplishments in which you will take part, defy description!

Many years ago, I propounded a theory that has since been repeated so often that it now sounds like a platitude. The fact remains, however, that the truth of my statement is being proved every day. What was that statement? Simply this:

Whatever the mind of man can conceive and believe, the mind can achieve!

Truly, my young friends, your future—your attainments and achievements—will be limited only by the limits of your imagination!

There is no doubt that each of you will experience disappointments and temporary setbacks. And there's no doubt either that collective tragedy—possibly in the form of war or depression—will afflict your generation as it did those that went before you.

But here I can offer you another truth from the science of personal achievement that was my pleasure to formulate during the past fifty years: that is, that every adversity carries with it the seed of an equivalent benefit. Let me repeat that: *Every adversity carries with it the seed of an equivalent benefit.*

It's Up to You

It's up to you, however, to find this seed, nurture it, and bring it to full growth and fruition. No one can do this for you. Each of us, with the help of our Almighty Creator, creates our own destiny. And by like token, each of us must find those hidden benefits that he grants us in moments of adversity.

Let me repeat once more those two statements that I think form the pillars upon which you may, with faith, build the structure of a successful life. The first is, *whatever the mind of man can conceive and believe, the mind can achieve. Secondly, every adversity carries with it the seed of an equivalent benefit.*

If you master these two concepts, you will have taken two giant strides toward achieving happiness.

You have already set yourself on the road to success through the effort and work and perseverance you've demonstrated during the past four years. During this period, you have—with the splendid help of the Salem College faculty—prepared the soil of life's garden, cultivating and feeding it in preparation for planting.

Don't let anyone try to minimize the value of your college education. It has given you a tremendous advantage for shaping your future. Only as the years roll by will you come to the full realization of the help you have received from the fine men and women of the college staff. And with every passing year I'm sure you'll find reason for ever-greater gratitude toward them.

Now, with your graduation from Salem you are about to start planting the actual seeds from which you will reap a harvest later in life. There is one warning I would like to give you in this regard: Don't wait too long to start planting! Now, in the springtime of your life, is the time to decide exactly what sort of a harvest you want your life to yield. The longer you delay planting, the longer the harvest is delayed.

And this, my friends, brings me to the heart of my talk with you today.

I have been asked to tell you what I consider to be the five essential characteristics or traits that lead to success in life.

Why, you may ask, am I qualified to speak on this subject of success? I hope throughout your lifetime you will always keep the same questioning attitude regarding anyone who claims to speak with authority.

Well, Oliver Goldsmith once said that "you can preach a better sermon with your life than with your lips." So perhaps you'll indulge me for a moment if I state my qualifications to speak on the subject of personal achievement.

It was in 1908 that, as a young magazine writer, I came into contact with Andrew Carnegie, the great steel magnate. Much has been said and much has been written about Carnegie. Some of it has been derogatory. But let me tell you that during the course of a friendship that lasted through many years, I never knew a person of higher ideals, of warmer heart, or greater love for his fellow man.

Nowhere did he demonstrate this love more directly than in his suggestion that I take on the task of formulating a definite philosophy of human achievement. It was his hope that people such as you could avoid the haphazard trial-and-error method by which he rose to his high station.

As result of Mr. Carnegie's suggestion, and with his help, I spent twenty years interviewing hundreds of successful people in all walks of life.

Many of these people became my close personal friends. They included men such as Thomas Edison, Alexander Graham Bell, and Henry Ford.

Out of this research evolved what is known as the "science of success," based on seventeen principles which I found to be the deciding factors in bringing about an individual's success or failure.

Five Absolute Essentials of Success

Five of these principles will be presented to you today as absolute essentials of success. If properly applied, they can carry you from this point forward to wherever you desire to be in the calling of your choice.

I must remind you, however, that there is no such reality in this world as something for nothing. Everything worth having has a price upon it. As Emerson has so well stated: "Nothing can bring you peace but yourself. Nothing can bring you peace but the triumph of principles."

Paraphrasing this wise admonition, let us say that nothing can bring you success but yourself.

Nothing can bring you success but the application of the principles that have been responsible for all successes.

Let me list for you now the five essentials of success. They are:

1. Definiteness of Purpose
2. The Master Mind principle

3. Going the Extra Mile

4. Self-Discipline

5. Applied Faith

Definiteness of Purpose

All successful achievement starts with definiteness of purpose. No man may hope to succeed unless he knows precisely what he wants and conditions his mind to complete the action necessary to attain it.

How does one go about conditioning his mind with definiteness of purpose? Simply by cultivating a deep and enduring capacity for belief!

I could cite example after example to prove that definiteness of purpose pays off. But I can think of no better case than that of Mr. W. Clement Stone of Chicago.

Shortly after my book *Think and Grow Rich* was published, Mr. Stone came across a copy of it. At that time, he was earning a modest living as an insurance salesman. That was in 1938.

As a result of what my book said about the need to choose a definite goal in life, Mr. Stone took a notebook from his pocket and wrote the following words: "My goal in life is this: By 1956 I will be president of the biggest exclusive old-line legal reserve health and accident insurance company in the world."

Mr. Stone signed his name to this and began reading it over to himself daily until it was seared into his consciousness. And because he knew what he wanted, he was able to recognize opportunity when it came his way. When the chance came for him to acquire the Combined Insurance Company of America, he was able to act with swift determination toward accomplishing his goal. And through his energy, the firm has now become what he determined it would be—the biggest exclusive accident and health firm in the world.

Now, I might add, Mr. Stone devotes much of his time and talent to helping others achieve their goals—by sponsoring the Science of Success home study course and by publishing a monthly magazine, *Success Unlimited*.

Mr. Stone became successful because he knew what he wanted, believed he would get it, and stood by that belief until it produced the opportunities he needed to fulfill his purpose.

There is something about the power of thought that seems to attract to a person the material equivalent of his aims and purposes. This power is not man-made. But it was made for man to use, and to enable him to control much of his earthly destiny.

In essence, we enter this world with the equivalent of a sealed envelope containing a long list of blessings each of us may enjoy by embracing and using the power of our minds. But the envelope also contains a list of penalties to be paid by the person who neglects to recognize this power and use it.

This gift is the only thing any of us controls absolutely. Therefore, it's the most precious thing we possess.

Just remember this: Whatever it is you possess, you must use it wisely—or lose it. And this, of course, includes your inexorable right to establish your own purpose in life and to keep your mind fixed on that purpose until you attain it.

Remember, also, that you can hit no higher than you aim. Therefore, don't be afraid to aim high—very high.

Which reminds me of the time the great evangelist, Dwight Moody, joined another minister in asking a wealthy lady for her contribution to a building fund. Before entering her mansion, Moody asked the other minister what amount they should request of the woman.

"Oh," said the pastor, "about $250."

"I think you'd better let me handle this," Moody replied.

When he met the lady, Moody said flatly: "We've come to ask you for two thousand dollars toward building a new mission."

The lady threw up her hands in horror and said: "Oh, Mr. Moody! I couldn't possibly give more than one thousand dollars."

Moody and the minister walked away with a check in that amount.

The point of this story, of course, is that life will give you young people no more than you demand of it. You may not achieve all that you hope to. But unless you choose a definite major purpose in life, you cannot hope to achieve *anything*!

Remember, too, that your goal need not involve the accumulation of material wealth.

Men like Albert Schweitzer, Jonas Salk, and Father Damien have achieved their definite major purposes. And in not one of these cases was it their purpose to acquire so much as a single dollar for the money itself. Indeed, I can think of no greater way for any of you to gain happiness and peace of mind during your lifetime than to set yourself a specific goal for serving your fellow human beings.

On the other hand, let me emphasize that there is no conflict between wealth and a state of spiritual peace of mind. Wealth, honestly acquired, is a great blessing—and especially so when the wealthy person thinks of himself as a steward who can use his funds to help others.

In selecting your goal, remember that nothing is impossible in this day when, as Rodgers and Hammerstein said in *Cinderella*, "Impossible things are happening every day."

As a news reporter, I covered the efforts of the Wright Brothers at Arlington, Virginia, to convince the Navy they had a machine that could fly.

For three days I sat in my automobile as Orville and Wilbur Wright endeavored to get their plane into the air. Finally, it rose for a few seconds, then came down with a crash and appeared broken to pieces.

An elderly gentleman standing nearby said: "They'll never make them thar things fly, will they, son? If God had wanted man to fly, he would have given him wings, wouldn't he?"

At the time, it appeared the old man was right. But I wonder what that gentleman would have said if, a few days ago, he could have sat with me in a modern airliner, flying at more than three hundred miles an hour, nearly five miles above the earth, calmly eating lunch?

How can you master the first of the five essentials of success?

Decide soon—within the next few weeks, if possible—upon a definite major purpose in your life. Write it down clearly and in detail in a pocket-sized notebook. Sign it, memorize it, and repeat it aloud at least three times daily in affirmation of your belief that it can be achieved.

In the same notebook, write out a clear description of the plan by which you intend to achieve your goal. State the maximum of time in which you intend to achieve it. Also, describe in detail precisely why you believe you will attain your purpose and what you intend to give in return for it. This latter is important. Give it much thought.

Keep your goal constantly before you.

Keep your goal constantly before you so that your subconscious mind can work on it through auto-suggestion.

And above all, don't forget to seek guidance in prayer. Throughout your lifetime, your spirit must grow apace with your body. Prayer and work go hand in hand to bring us peace of mind.

This was illustrated when the head of a monastery heard a monk express doubt about the order's motto: "Pray and work." He invited the young man to go rowing with him and took the oars himself.

After a while, the young man pointed out that the superior was using only one oar and said: "If you don't use both, we'll just go around in circles and you won't get anywhere."

"That's right, my son," the elder man replied. "One oar is called prayer and the other is called work. Unless you use both at the same time, you just go in circles and you don't get anywhere."

The seasoning influence of the years on my life has brought me into a better understanding of the attitude in which to go to prayer. As a result, I now always close my prayer with these words:

Oh Infinite Intelligence, I ask not for more blessings, but more wisdom with which to make better use of the greatest of all blessings with which I was endowed at birth—the right to embrace and direct to ends of my own choice the powers of my mind.

The Master Mind

This brings us to the second of the five essentials of success, known as the *Master Mind* principle. It consists simply of an alliance of two or more persons who coordinate their efforts in a spirit of perfect harmony for the attainment of a definite purpose.

It was Andrew Carnegie who first introduced me to this principle when I asked him to describe the means by which he had accumulated his great fortune. He answered frankly that it came through the efforts of other men—the men who belong to his Master Mind group. Then, one by one, he named the members of the group and what each contributed to its success.

Carnegie made clear to me that while any individual can achieve success, far greater success can be achieved through a group working in perfect harmony so that their talents, education, and personalities complement one another.

The Declaration of Independence was created by the most profound Master Mind alliance this nation has ever known. It consisted of the fifty-six brave men who signed the document, knowing that they were risking both their lives and their fortunes. Here was perfect harmony at its highest level—and its results have, to a large extent, changed the destiny of the entire human race.

There are three points of contact at which I urge you to relate yourself with others on the Master Mind basis: in your home, in your church, and in your place of occupation or business. Do this faithfully and you will have gone a long way toward insuring your prosperity, peace of mind, and sound health.

Time and again I have seen how the Master Mind alliance— the group working in harmony—produces astounding results.

Could one man, for example, ever have accomplished the scientific work that resulted in production of atomic power? Never! Each of us can accomplish only so much in a single lifetime. But by working in a harmony with others toward a single goal, results that normally would take centuries can be achieved in a relatively short time.

Going the Extra Mile

The third of the five essentials of success is the habit of *Going the Extra Mile*. In the Sermon on the Mount, we are told: "If any man requires you to go with him one mile, go with him twain."

The habit of going the extra mile merely means the practice of rendering more and better service than you are paid to render—and doing it in a positive, pleasing attitude.

I have never known a single person to achieve outstanding success without following the habit of rendering more service than was expected of him.

And I wish to cite you the record of a man whom I first met here at Salem College when I delivered the commencement address thirty-five years ago. He is a man who is well known to all of you. Of course, I'm speaking of Jennings Randolph, who, I should add, is known affectionately in my organization as "Mr. Courtesy."

After completing his work at Salem College, Jennings was elected to Congress, where he served the people of West Virginia for fourteen years. And I wish to tell you just one of the ways in which he followed the habit of going the extra mile.

During the summer, after Congress adjourned and most other congressmen had returned to their homes to attend to private affairs, Jennings remained at his office in Washington, maintaining his staff as usual in order to be of continuous service to his constituents.

He didn't have to do this. It wasn't expected of him. Nor did he get extra pay for doing it—that is, no pay that came in his government paycheck.

All successful achievement starts with definiteness of purpose. No man may hope to succeed unless he knows precisely what he wants and conditions his mind to complete the action necessary to attain it.

But there came a day when this habit of going beyond the letter of responsibility began to pay off handsomely. This habit brought him to the attention of the president of Capital Airlines, who appointed him as assistant to the president and director of public relations for Capital.

Thirty-five years ago, Jennings Randolph heard me describe the benefits one may receive by going the extra mile when I delivered my first Salem College commencement address. He was impressed by what he heard. He was ready for the message. Then and there he declared his intention of embracing this principle and applying it in all of his human relationships.

Jennings Randolph has prospered and his friends are legion throughout this nation because he recognized that whatever we do to or for another, we do to or for ourselves—that no useful service can be rendered without its just reward, albeit the reward may not come back from the source to which we delivered the service.

"Men suffer all their life long," said Emerson, "under the foolish superstition that they can be cheated. But it is as impossible for a man to be cheated by anyone but himself, as for a thing to be, and not to be, at the same time. There is a third silent party to all our bargains. The nature and soul of things takes on itself the guaranty of fulfillment of every contract, so that honest service cannot come to loss. If you serve an ungrateful master, serve him the more. Every stroke shall be repaid. The longer the payment is withholding, the better for you; for compound interest on compound interest is the rate and usage of this exchequer."

When Paul Harris graduated from law school, he was confronted with the problem of building a clientele.

He had never heard of the principle of *Going the Extra Mile*, as such. But he put the principle to work so effectively that he lived to see the day when he turned away more prospective clients he could not serve than those he accepted.

His plan was simple. He invited a group of business and professional men to meet with him at luncheon weekly in what he called the Rotary Club. The original purpose of the club was to inspire its members to patronize one another and to induce outsiders to patronize members of the club.

The plan worked so successfully that Rotary is now an international institution with influences for the betterment of mankind all over the world. There is nothing to hinder you young men who contemplate entering a profession from adopting Paul Harris's principle and giving it an application that can increase your acquaintanceship and build goodwill for you as it did for him.

Self-Discipline

The fourth essential for success is *Self-Discipline*. That means mastery of self over both the mental faculties and the physical body. Self-discipline begins with a burning desire to become the master of one's self. The motivation necessary to keep that desire alert and active is recognition of the fact that when one becomes master of himself, he may become the master over many things—including the failures and defeats and problems that we encounter along the way.

Another inspiring motive that should keep the burning desire for self-mastery alive is recognition of the true significance of the gift from the Creator of one's unchallengeable right to control and direct his own mind.

Milo C. Jones worked a small farm near Fort Atkinson, Wisconsin. His hours were long, the work was hard, and every member of his family had to help in order to make ends meet.

Then disaster struck. Milo was stricken down by double paralysis and totally deprived of the use of his body. His farming days were over forever.

His family rolled him out in a wheelchair on the porch each day, where he sat in the sun while other members of the family carried on with the farmwork.

One morning, some three weeks after he was stricken, he made a stupendous discovery. He discovered that he had a mind.

Inasmuch as his mind was the only thing he had left with which he could exercise any sort of discipline, he began to put it to work. As a result, he came up with an idea that brought him and his family happiness and wealth.

Calling his family around him, he said, "I want you to plant every acre of our land in corn. Start raising hogs on this corn, and while they are still young and tender, slaughter them and make them into 'Little Pig Sausage.'"

"Little Pig Sausage" became a household word all over America, and Milo C. Jones lived to see his brainchild make him a very rich man. Although he learned very late, he made the discovery that I trust each of you young people will make early in your career: he discovered that there are no limitations to the power of the mind except those which one sets up for himself through doubts, fears, and lack of ambition or definiteness of purpose.

Your first duty in forming the habit of self-discipline is to try to win full and complete control of your own mind and direct it to definite objectives from which you may gain wisdom as well as material and spiritual prosperity.

Then you will need discipline over the emotion of anger. This you can attain by recognizing that no one can make you angry without your full consent and cooperation. You do not need to give that cooperation.

You will need discipline over your sex emotions, by learning the art of transmuting this profound creative force into channels that will aid you in the calling you have chosen.

You will need discipline over your tone of voice so as to make it gentle, yet convincing.

You will need discipline over everything you take into your physical body in the form of food, and drink, and drugs, and alcohol, and smokes. Remember, your body is God's temple, given you as a house for the protection of your mind and soul.

You will need discipline over your choice of personal associates.

You will need discipline over your thought habits, by keeping your mind busily occupied in thinking and planning for the things and circumstances you desire and off of those you do not desire.

You will need discipline to avoid procrastination.

You will need discipline over the emotion of love. If you love without your love being returned, be satisfied that *you* are the one who has gained most because the expression of love has added refinements to your soul. Therefore, don't waste time over unrequited love—and perish the idea that one can love but once.

You will need to discipline yourself to recognize that whatever happens to you, be it good or bad, most likely had its cause somewhere within you—either by your thoughts, deeds, or your neglect to act.

This is quite an order that I have given you.

But you can fill it if you are interested enough in your future to do so. By the time you will have filled this order you will know yourself, your potentials for success, your weaknesses, and your strengths. And you will be in a position to make the most of the prerogative your Creator has given you to control both your mind and your body.

Applied Faith

This brings us to the fifth and the last of the five essentials of success. It is called *Applied Faith*—the sort of faith that one backs with deeds as well as belief.

Faith is a state of mind that has been called "the mainspring of the soul," and it is that through which one's aims, desires, plans, and purposes may be translated into their material equivalent.

Faith begins with the recognition of the existence and the inexorable powers of Infinite Intelligence.

There is no such reality as a blanket faith based upon an unproven hypothesis.

Faith is guidance! It won't of itself bring you the things you desire. But it can and will show you the path by which you may go after those things.

Through faith you can do anything you believe you can do, provided only that it harmonizes with natural laws.

When Dr. Frank W. Gunsaulus was a young preacher on Chicago's South Side, his following was small, his income meager. But he had long cherished the idea of building a new type of educational institution where the students would devote half their time to "book learning," the other half to applying this training in the laboratory of practical experience.

He needed a million dollars to start the project. So he asked for guidance through prayer. His efforts brought him immediate and dramatic results—an idea he believed would give him the money he needed.

He wrote a sermon entitled "What I Would Do with a Million Dollars" and announced in the Chicago newspapers that he would preach a sermon on that subject the following Sunday.

That Sunday morning, before he left his home for his church, he knelt down and offered the most fervent prayer he had ever expressed, requesting that the notice of his sermon would come to the attention of someone who could provide the money he sought.

Then he rushed to his church. As he was ascending the pulpit, however, he discovered that he had left his carefully prepared sermon at home—too far away to be recovered in time to deliver it.

"Right then and there," said Dr. Gunsaulus, "I offered another prayer, and in a matter of seconds, the answer I desired came. It said, 'Go into your pulpit and tell your audience of your plan, and tell it with all of your enthusiasm your soul can muster.'"

Dr. Gunsaulus did just that. He described the sort of school he had long wished to organize, how he wished to operate it, the sort of benefits it would render its students, and the amount of money he needed to get it going.

Those who heard the sermon said he never spoke like that before and never again thereafter, for he was speaking as an inspired man with a burning desire to render a great service.

At the end of his sermon, a stranger arose from the rear of the church, walked slowly down the aisle, whispered something in the minister's ear, then slowly walked back to his seat.

There was absolute silence.

Then Dr. Gunsaulus said, "My friends, you have just witnessed one of God's miracles. The gentleman who just walked down the aisle and spoke to me is Philip D. Armour. He told me if I would come down to his office, he would arrange for me to have the million dollars I need for the school."

The donation built the Armour School of Technology, of which Dr. Gunsaulus became the head. In recent years, the school has become part of the Illinois Institute of Technology.

"The mystery of the whole thing," said Dr. Gunsaulus, "was why I waited so long before going to the proper source for the solution of my problem."

That same mystery has confused many other people who have delayed going to prayer until after everything else had failed to bring the desired results in times of need and emergency.

And this may be one reason why prayer so often brings only negative results, as it generally does when one goes to prayer without true faith, after having met with disaster, or when disaster seems imminent.

I have received an impressive lesson on the power of prayer when my second son was born without ears.

The doctors broke the news to me as gently as possible, hoping to soften the shock. They ended the announcement by saying, "Of course, your son will always be a deaf-mute because no one born like him has ever learned to hear or to speak."

*Whatever the mind can conceive and believe,
the mind can achieve.*

There was a mighty fine opportunity for me to test my faith, and I did it by telling the doctors that while I had not seen my son, there was one thing of which I was very sure—that he would not go through life as a deaf-mute.

One of the doctors walked over, laid his hand on my shoulder, and said, "Now look here, Napoleon, there are some things in this world that neither you nor anyone else can do anything about, and this is one of them."

"There is nothing I can't do something about," I replied, "if it is no more than relate myself to an unfortunate circumstance so as to prevent it from breaking my heart."

I went to work on my son through prayer before I saw him, and I kept this up many hours daily. After three years, it became obvious that he was hearing. How much he heard we did not know.

But by the time he was nine years old he had developed sixty-five percent of his normal hearing capacity. That was enough to get him through the grade schools, high school, and to the third year in the University of West Virginia, when the Acousticon Company built him an electrical hearing aid that gave him his full, one hundred percent hearing capacity—just what I told the doctors would happen.

Out of that experience came my motto "Whatever the mind can conceive and believe, the mind can achieve." I wrote that motto literally in tears of sorrow, under emotional strain that tore at my heartstrings.

And somehow I can never dismiss the thought that this experience has been the richest of my entire life, because it brought me safely through a testing time from which I learned that our only limitations are those that we set up and accept in our minds.

I have now given you what I consider the five essentials of success. You may use them, if you choose to unlock the door to your desired goal in life.

Great as has been our scientific advances in the thirty-five years since I last appeared here, I look for still greater progress in the coming three-and-a-half decades. But these advances won't be in the field of science alone. They will be in the field of humanity itself.

A new spirit is sweeping the world in spite of the dark fears raised by the threat of nuclear warfare. Man is indeed learning that he is his brother's keeper! We are advancing not only in the material realm, but in the realm of the spirit. Never in the history of mankind have so many persons devoted their time and energy and wealth to helping other men and women.

There are no better goals for you young people than to join the ranks of these altruists.

Remember that we do not *find* happiness; we make it. And by like token, the things you sell for a price are gone forever, while the things you give away with your sincere blessings come back to you greatly multiplied.

Christianity has become one of the great forces of civilization because its founder paid for it with his life and gave it to the world with his blessings.

In the spirit of brotherly love, which he taught, I have brought you this message with the hope that it may help smooth the path of your lives and bring you nearer to your chosen goals.